MY TESTIMONY!

by

LACY MEGAN [MIDKIFF] MARTINEZ

authorHOUSE®

AuthorHouse™
1663 Liberty Drive
Bloomington, IN 47403
www.authorhouse.com
Phone: 1 (800) 839-8640

Scripture quotations marked KJV are from the Holy Bible, King James Version (Authorized Version). First published in 1611. Quoted from the KJV Classic Reference Bible, Copyright © 1983 by The Zondervan Corporation.

Published by AuthorHouse   07/21/2015

ISBN: 978-1-5049-1044-6 (sc)
ISBN: 978-1-5049-1043-9 (e)

Library of Congress Control Number: 2015906764

Print information available on the last page.

Any people depicted in stock imagery provided by Thinkstock are models, and such images are being used for illustrative purposes only.
Certain stock imagery © Thinkstock.

This book is printed on acid-free paper.

DEDICATION

This book is dedicated to my Lord and Savior, Jesus Christ, in whom I am nothing without. Also to God, my Father in Heaven and the Holy Spirit, who leads me and guides me into all truth and righteousness.

FOREWORD

Lacy Martinez is a creative writer and uses her gift of writing as an opportunity to share with you her personal journey and experience through this thing called, "Life". She invites you to take this adventure with her and be encouraged by how the Lord can lead and guide you in practical ways and in every day life. She shares with you how even in the most mundane, boring days and in the hard, challenging days, God can speak to you and do incredible things in your life. Lacy hopes you are encouraged as you read her book and discover that there is more to this life than you can imagine!

INTRODUCTION

My name is Lacy Megan Martinez, maiden name Midkiff. I am 31 years old. I am a Christian and in love with Jesus! This book is about my walk and testimony of what God, Jesus, and the Holy Spirit have done in my life. This is my personal testimony. Revelation 12:11 KJV says, "And they overcame him by the blood of the Lamb, and by the word of their testimony; and they loved not their lives unto the death." The Lord asked me to write a book about my testimony. I truly believe and have a sincere hope that as you read my book, you will be encouraged and able to overcome the things that are holding you back or weighing you down. I hope this book helps you to realize that you can overcome, too!

CONTENTS

Chapter One

"THE BEGINNING"

It was in the emergency operating room where I was born and took my first breath. I was delivered by cesarean. I was a month late from my due date and my Mom had to have an emergency c-section. The umbilical cord was wrapped around my neck twice so the Doctor had to get me out quick. I survived by God's grace! He kept me alive to live and proclaim His goodness. I was a huge baby, weighing in at nine pounds and five ounces. My parents were just happy that I was alive after that traumatizing event. The devil wanted me dead from the beginning, but I was a fighter! I was going to live and tell others my testimony.

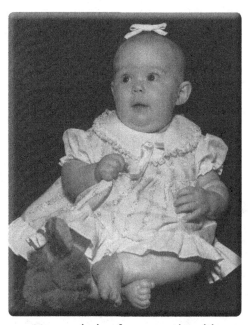

Me as a baby- four months old.

The first 10 years of my life were nothing special. I was born in Panorama City, California on Thursday, November 10th, 1983. I grew up in "The Valley", which was Reseda, California. I went to Pre-school at St. Martin's, where my Mother was a Pre-school teacher. I attended Kindergarten there for two years. Yes, two years! I was held back for another year because I was too young to move on to First Grade at this specific school. I had a best friend named Tori Victor. We went to school together and we were best friends outside of school.

Me in Kindergarden with my school uniform on.

When I was about to start First Grade my parents decided to move about an hour North up to the Mojave Desert to a place called, "The Antelope Valley". Our specific city in the Antelope Valley was called, "Palmdale". When we moved I was devastated. I did not want to leave my best friend, Tori. I also didn't want to go to a new place and start First Grade at a new school. I started First Grade at Cottonwood Elementary. I remember crying when I got there. I was still so sad and devastated. I remember my Mom leaving me while I was crying. I knew I'd be okay, but it was a lot to adjust to at five years old.

Me in roller skates being silly!

My Dad wanted to move to a newer area that was growing and developing. He started his own business there in Lancaster, California. His business was called, "Dimples Family Fun Center". It was an indoor mini golf course, a ball crawl, and had games and food. So, for the next seven years of my life I would pretty much spend all of my time (outside of school) at work with them. I felt like I lived there sometimes. I even had my own cot to sleep on in the back room.

I remember they worked there almost all the time. Both of my parents would work open to close and sometimes through the night to do inventory. I would just sleep there while they worked. Some kids and friends of mine thought it was so awesome for me to have cool parents that owned a fun place like this, but for me it wasn't so fun. I did have fun playing there and having my parties and girls sleepovers there, but sometimes I just wanted to be home and have my parents to myself. I got tired of being at Dimples all the time. This was pretty much my life when I was a child; school and Dimples. So, like I said for seven years, between the age of five and 12, I would basically be a regular kid, going to regular school, and spending the rest of my time at my parent's work.

I was an only child this whole time. My Mom never wanted to have any more kids after me since her emergency delivery was horrific. It instilled so much fear in her that she was too scared to do it again. My parents had talked about maybe some day adopting more kids when I was older, but for now I was a lone ranger. This led to a lot of boredom when I was at home. My parents were usually busy so I had to keep myself occupied by reading or playing Barbies. Don't get me wrong, I do have some good memories of my Dad playing outside with me and my Mom taking me shopping. You know when you are a kid though, you just feel like you need them to be with you every second. I felt like mine were busy working most of the time. I felt lonely a lot.

From that lonely feeling, I would often just sit on my bed and talk to God. I had never been to church and had never been taught about God, but something inside me knew He was real and that He was there. I would say, "God, I know you are up in Heaven. I know You are real. My name is Lacy Megan Midkiff and I live at 40423 Elderberry Court in "Palmdale, California..." I would just tell Him about myself (as if He didn't already know) and just talk to Him and ask Him questions.

Me in First Grade, six years old.

Like I said, I had never been to church my whole life and I was already 10 years old now when things started to get interesting. Now, my parents were good people. They didn't cheat, didn't steal, didn't lie, etc. They taught me to be truthful, trustworthy, faithful, hard-working, etc., but there was something that my parents were still missing in their life. Despite their good efforts, their own thriving business, and the perfect child they had (haha), there was a certain emptiness that they felt. They had a feeling of unfulfillment.

CHAPTER TWO

"THE NEED FOR JESUS"

At 10 years old I remember my Mom struggling with anxiety attacks. She would, at different times, start to experience what we would call a "panic attack". She would go out to a store, say Target for example, and as she would enter that store she would become fearful. Her heart would start to hurt and race faster than it should. She would get nervous and think she was having a heart attack. Her breathing became harder and she couldn't take it anymore. We would have to leave the store before we even began our shopping. After this same thing repeated over and over again wherever she would go, she finally sought professional help. She started seeing a therapist once a week. After weeks of counseling the therapist did not know what else to do to help her so he recommended that maybe she should try going to church. He told her maybe a good church would help. He recommended her two different churches that he knew were good churches. One of the churches he told her about was "Harvest Christian Church", and the other one was also a Christian church, whose name I can't remember now.

My Mom thought about it and taking the idea of "church" into consideration, she came home to tell my Dad what he had said. Now, there was no way on the earth my Dad wanted to go to church. "Church, no, that's not for me", he would say. I was in agreement with him. I would think, "Church? Why do we need to go to church? For what? All church is, is another frivolous activity to take time away from our weekend! No thanks!" But with "church" being a final option for my Mom, my Dad decided to do it just for my Mom's sake. He told me secretly, "I know you and I both don't want to go, but we need to try to go at least one time and see if it helps Mom". So, begrudgingly, we both went with my Mom that following Sunday. We chose Harvest Church because a friend of my Dad's had also mentioned that same church to him during a conversation that week. Coincidence? No.

We went and my Mom really liked the church. She felt accepted and she was invited to a women's meeting/Bible study. She attended the Bible study that following week, hesitating as she was going because she was scared and still having anxiety. My Dad took her and had urge her to go into the room. A lady was there that worked in the office and she noticed my Mom's hesitation and nervousness. She talked with my Mom and tried to make her feel comfortable and put her at ease. She told my Mom about this person named Jesus and how He came to die for our sins and to set us free from things like anxiety. After a lengthy discussion, she led my Mom to the Lord! So, what does that mean? It means that this lady shared with my Mom about how to come to the Lord and accept His salvation for us. Turning away from our sin and acknowledging that we need Him to save us from ourselves and asking Him to be Lord of our lives is how we come to Jesus. This lady was just the instrument God used to help lead my Mom to that place.

My Mom said the "Sinner's Prayer" with this lady. The "Sinner's Prayer" is a prayer to God. It meant that she confessed her sins to God, asked Jesus to come into her heart and forgive her of her sins, and she asked Him to come be Lord of her life! After giving Jesus her burdens and asking Him to free her from her anxiety, she did, in fact, feel so free. She felt the fear leave her. God healed her of her anxiety. She went back to join the women's Bible study and they started teaching her what it meant to be a Christian. My Dad picked her up after it was over and she told him about what had happened and about "this lady," and about accepting Jesus. He was kind of like, "Okay, whatever works for you." He didn't really understand the whole Jesus thing and giving Him our life. He was just happy that my Mom was okay.

Immediately after that, she started changing. She was free to go to the store now, without being afraid she would have a heart attack. My Dad and I started seeing a change in her. Watching her go from this scared, fearful person into a completely free person right away really started making my Dad and I question what this whole Jesus thing and church thing was about. There was a class at this church called, "The New Believer's Class" and my Mom wanted to go to it. She asked my Dad to come with her. He went to the class with her and the Pastor did a demonstration about what it means to put Jesus in charge of your life. He showed a drawing of how we are on the throne and we rule our lives and then how there are other smaller thrones beneath us where Jesus is or our spouse is, etc. He taught that becoming a Christian means you give Jesus your life and you put Him on the throne and how you allow Him to rule and lead your life. You choose to move yourself beneath Him and you let Him take "center stage", so to speak.

Two weeks later, my Dad accepted Jesus in his heart! In the shower, he prayed and said, "God, if you are real, let me know You are real." He said he could literally feel an awesome presence like warm oil come over him and start at the top of his head and go down to the toes of his feet. It was like a cleansing coming over him, getting rid of everything that was a burden to him. No, it was not the hot water, it was God's presence! That illustration that the Pastor gave finally clicked in his brain and he understood what it meant. He chose to make Jesus Lord of his life and put Him on the throne! After he made this choice, I could see a difference in him as well.

That got me thinking and I began to see what Jesus can do in my own parent's lives. I liked how they seemed more joyful and carefree. At this same time they had another Dimples open in Bakersfield, California and it was not doing so well. They were about to lose everything and it was going to close down. I saw the fear my Dad had from that thought of losing everything turn to joy and trust in the Lord. Because he had now made Jesus Lord of his life he didn't have to worry anymore. He trusted God to take care of us and our family even if they did lose everything.

So, with that being said, just two weeks after he accepted Jesus into his heart (right around the time of my eleventh birthday), I got down on my knees in my bedroom and prayed "The Prayer of Salvation"! I too asked Jesus into my heart. I asked Him to forgive me of my sins. I repented. I asked Him to be Lord of my life. I gave Him my heart. I wanted Jesus to be my Savior. That night, in my room alone, is when I officially became a "Christian." I then wanted my life to please Him. I wanted to live for Him and I wanted to read the Bible and learn about Him. My whole view on going to church changed. I wanted to go now. I wanted to make other Christian friends that felt the same way I did. I started getting involved in the youth group at this church. I started going to youth Bible study on Wednesday night. I read the Bible at home and my parents and I talked about the Scriptures whenever we could. We were all a newly "saved" family learning the way of a Christian together.

Two months later, in the cold of January, I, and both of my parents, were baptized together by our Pastor's wife! It was a wonderful time to publicly declare Jesus Lord of our lives and to confess Him as our Savior. From this moment on I have been seeking God's will for my life, reading and studying the Bible, memorizing Scripture, telling others about Jesus, and learning how to trust the Lord in everything! I was now 11 years old and so thankful that I was a "born again" believer who could now serve the Lord and be saved from my sin. I didn't have to worry about going to Hell because I had salvation from Jesus! I was redeemed!

CHAPTER THREE

"THE TEENAGE YEARS"

I wasn't ever a "bad kid" or a "rebellious teenager," but I did have an attitude and was sarcastic sometimes. I had to work on my attitude. There wasn't anything "really bad" that I ever got in to. I never did drugs, never partied, never drank, didn't cuss, didn't watch rated R movies, wasn't into fornication, etc. I never did any of this before I was saved, but having the Holy Spirit in me helped me to be even stronger now! As I got older and because I didn't do those things I was often called a "Goody Two Shoes," (whatever that means) or a "Teacher's Pet." I just tried to always do what was right and did my best at whatever I did. I got straight A's in school and was never in trouble. I always liked going to school and working hard, until I started Junior High. I started Junior High after I accepted Jesus into my heart.

I started Junior High when I was 11 (almost 12). When I first started Junior High I liked it. I had friends from Elementary School that came to the same Junior High I did. I was getting straight A's. I was working hard and making my parents and teachers proud! As the school year went along and I became more mature in my walk with Jesus, I started noticing all the evil around me. I viewed things from a different perspective now; from a Christian perspective. I knew I was living for something bigger than myself now. Things my friends were talking about and doing started to bother me. In my Science class we started learning about evolution. I had to start sticking up for my faith and expressing to the teacher that what he was teaching was wrong and that it was a lie.

As far as being around my friends at school, they could see I was quiet when they talked. I didn't engage in their conversations about things I didn't think were right or good to talk about. Do you know what happened then? My "friends" turned on me, forsook me, and started to ignore me. They didn't understand why I was different now. It bothered them that I wasn't talking like them and doing what they were doing. I was also the kind of person that didn't care about name brands. I would get my shoes at Payless because I liked them and they were cheap. I didn't care. Most teenagers at my school had the name brand shoes. If you didn't have name brand shoes, then you just weren't cool. That didn't bother me, but it bothered other people because I wasn't conforming to what they thought I needed to have. I think what bothered them most is the fact that I was secure and content with who I was and I didn't need name brand shoes to be my security. For some of these girls and most guys, they had to have the name brand shoes as their security and to fit in.

I specifically remember one girl asking me where I got my shoes at. When I told her, "Payless", she was so angry with me and told me they weren't cool and that I was basically a loser and that I needed to buy name brand shoes to fit in. I could tell that it bothered her that I didn't get bothered by her telling me that. I felt so bad for her. Even though I was only in Junior High it was so sad to me to see how badly these girls and boys would do anything just to fit in among their peers. They would go under the bleachers and make out with someone just to have a "cool" status. These were 11 and 12 year olds!

Even though we were all still so young, not really even teenagers yet, I started hearing so much cussing and swearing. I hated hearing it all the time. I would hear gossip. I would hear about who did what with their boyfriend and how so and so were making out, or as they called it back then "scamming" under the bleachers. And at 11 years old! Can you believe it? I couldn't believe it. I hated being around it. Yes, I was a girl with emotions and feelings and sure I had crushes on boys and all that, but I was never into dating or getting physical with guys at this age! I would never even let myself go there. The more and more I went to school, the less I wanted to be there. Every day I went I hated it it. All the drama and peer pressure and things I saw from this world started bothering me so much and making me sad and upset that I would come home crying. I was also in disbelief at what was already happening and going on in Junior High. Things you might expect in High School, but not Junior High were already happening in 6th grade! I thought if this is bad already, how much worse will it be for me in High School? It's not that I was scared to share my faith, but when I did share it I wasn't understood. I was also pretty timid and shy and just didn't know what to say at times.

I started begging my parents to let me stay home. I started begging my Mom to homeschool me. I wanted out! I just wanted to know Jesus and get away from all the stuff that was trying to pull me down eight hours every day. After months of coming home crying, begging, and pleading with my parents to homeschool me, they finally took me out of school and my Mom looked into homeschooling me. I think this was around January or February of that same school year. I started doing homeschool through a Christian curriculum at home. I did this for the remainder of my sixth grade year and all the way through eighth grade until I graduated from Junior High.

During these crucial beginning teenage years I stayed home a lot to do my schoolwork. On my free time I would read and pray over whatever chapter we were on that week in our youth Bible study at church. I would then write about what God had showed me and the revelation He would give me as I read His word. One time as I was about to write my study for that week, something came over me and I started shaking and my hand started writing so fast. I don't even know how I wrote so fast. I wrote out like five pages in a matter of minutes! Everything I wrote was like total revelation from the Lord. When I got to church I told the Pastor's wife about it because I was a little freaked out and not sure what had happened. She told me it was God's presence and spirit on me giving me the words to write. When it was my turn to share that night, all the youth started crying and repenting as I read what I wrote. There was not a dry eye in the room. It was so awesome to see God use me to do something like that. There would be more times like this to come! I would share the revelation He would give me at Bible study. In my "spare time", I would also sing Christian songs and practice my singing. I love to sing! I would listen to Christian audio books like "This Present Darkness" and learn about the spiritual realm. I would hang out with my Christian friends from church. I would clean. I loved cleaning the house for my Mom.

Then High School came around. I still did not want to go back to public school, but it was also getting hard for my Mom to homeschool me. She didn't know how to teach me certain things, especially math. She put me on Independent Study through the High School by our house called, "Highland High School". Independent Study is kind of like homeschooling. It is where you take all your work home with you for the week and do it at home. Then you go to school once a week for two hours to a special room and turn in all your work and take tests on the computer. I did this for the 9th grade and 10th grade years. I didn't even like going to school that one day a week, but it was better than all the time. Since I continued doing my work at home, I had more free time to pray, read my Bible, and study the Bible, just like I had done during my Junior High years. I really liked that! I would still study and write out what I learned from each chapter I read and bring it to our Wednesday night youth Bible Study.

There was also a Thursday morning women's Bible study that my Mom attended. She asked if I could go with her or else she wouldn't be able to come. It was supposed to be only for ladies 18 years and older only, but the women's Pastor and the lady's that attended felt that I was very mature for my age and allowed me to come! I started coming at 13 years old (I believe). I would also do my Bible study for this group and share during the meetings. I loved this time because I got to go to three classes every week and learn the Bible. Sundays to Sunday school youth group, Wednesdays to youth Bible study, and Thursdays to the women's Bible study. I was able to just jump in the Bible and study it, read it, teach it, and be taught it. This was a great time in my life of really learning the Bible fresh for the first time and getting to learn what a Christian really is. So, for the rest of my sixth grade year through 10th grade, this was pretty much my life, for five years. I think I loved every minute of my life. There was nothing better to me than to learn God's word and be excited about the truths in the Bible. I got to be with Christian friends and do school at home and really get a strong foundation for my life!

We were at this church, Harvest Community Church, for about five years. From a little before I turned 11 to 15 1/2 I was at this church. My family and I were very involved in this church. It was the first church we had ever been to and the people there were like our family. We were so close to everyone that it was literally our family. Even though we weren't blood related, we were true brothers and sisters in Christ! I was on the church choir. I was on the youth newsletter team, the youth worship team, in two Bible studies, I helped with food outreaches, evangelism, etc. I loved being a part of this church. I learned so much during these five years. Our church family was so full of love. I was always blessed by the youth leaders and by our friends. This is the only church I have been in where I felt a real bond, love, a sense of community and family. I had great youth leaders that really mentored me, such as DeBorah Frazer and Reina Perez. There were more, but these two really took the time to invest in my life!

During the time at this church I also went to a camp every year called "Hume Lake." It was a week of nothing but fun and getting to know God. We would get up and have morning Bible study and/or worship even before breakfast. Then we would eat and then go to our morning worship and teaching session. Then we'd have group games, lunch, free time and an evening worship and teaching session. Then dinner, more free time, and then small group sessions in our cabins. It was so fun! We all came home from camp so on fire for God. I wish all that we learned and how fired up we were stayed with us, but for most youth after a couple days or weeks the fire was gone. Unfortunately, when we return to "life" and if we don't keep cultivating that fire and relationship with God, it will start to dwindle and may eventually die altogether.

I tried to keep that fire going once I got home each year. I kept reading my Bible and going to Bible studies. Since I was home schooled now, it was easier for me to keep myself set apart and unpolluted by the world since I wasn't in public school. All of my friends in youth group were in public school though, so it wasn't so easy for them. A lot of my friends got into sexual relationships and fornication. I think just about all my friends "backslid" as they say. They would cuss, go to parties, dress immodestly or just get into things they knew they shouldn't be getting into. I was always very blunt with the truth of God's word. If I saw a friend in youth group doing something unbiblical I would go to them and talk to them about it. I would remind them that it wasn't good what they were doing. Instead of my friends being receptive and thankful that I loved them enough to remind them of truth and happy that I took my time to be a friend to them, I was shunned. Those people I confronted were not thankful and did not think I loved them. They took what I confronted them with as I was better than them and they didn't like it. They got angry, distant and some even hated me. I did lose friends. I found out over those years that it was hard to keep a lot of close friends when I lived a life according to the Bible. I found that a lot of Christians don't completely surrender their life to Jesus and therefore don't obey Him and remain in their sin and don't want to be confronted by it.

I did have a couple close friends, but we still didn't agree on some things; like secular music. I didn't listen to secular music because I believe it infiltrates our minds with garbage. I had a strong conviction about it and I thought if it doesn't glorify God, then why listen to it. My friends thought secular music was okay. They would listen to it. They would justify listening to it by saying they were listening to the music only, not the words. Nobody can say that because the next thing you know, about a week later, you find yourself singing the words randomly in the shower. Even if you are not focusing on the words, you have a subconscious that hears them and picks up everything. So, sometimes I felt kind of like I was the only one (besides one other best friend I had) that really wanted to wholeheartedly live for and please Jesus. I cannot judge anyone's heart, as only God knows our hearts, but from the fruit I saw when I was with my friends it didn't seem like they were 100% interested in pleasing Jesus and doing God's will. It seemed like they were interested in attracting boys with provocative clothing, listening to secular music, sneaking out, going to parties, etc.

Something the Lord started showing me during those years is that He wanted me to be "Set Apart". He didn't want me to be like everyone else. He kept showing me the words "set apart" and Scriptures about being set apart. (Psalm 4:3 NKJV "But know that the Lord has set apart for Himself him who is godly; The Lord will hear when I call to Him." Acts 20:32 NLT "And now I entrust you to God and the message of his grace that is able to build you up and give you an inheritance with all those He has set apart for himself.") My friends and I even liked to sing and we were going to call our group, "Set Apart"! God also started showing me Scriptures about being "Chosen". I knew there was a lot ahead of me that God had for me to do and become. I knew I could only do it by being obedient to Him, by staying set apart, and remembering that He chose me for this time in history. This was probably between the ages of 13 and 15 when He was showing me these things.

Around the time I turned 15, my parents were feeling lead by God to leave this church. They weren't sure why. They felt that there were some things that just weren't right in the leadership. They didn't want to leave. I didn't necessarily want to leave, either, but I was okay with it. This was our church family and we loved everyone! This is the place where we met Jesus. It was bitter-sweet to leave. Bitter to leave everyone we called "family", but sweet to obey God and see what was new that He had for us.

I need to throw this in here real quick. We had friends at this church that did foster care. They had a little girl that was up for adoption, but they didn't feel led to adopt her. They found out that she also had a brother that was up for adoption who was in a different foster home. My parents had looked into doing foster care so that they could adopt kids. They asked me what I felt about it and I told them I was fine with it. I didn't care and I even thought it would be nice to have a brother(s) and a sister(s). They took their foster care classes and got approved to do foster care. They had liked our friend's little girl and thought about adopting her. They prayed about taking in her brother, too. My Dad felt like the Lord told him to adopt the boy and my parents both felt led to adopt the girl. The fosters parents that had the girl at this time were in agreement with my parents and thought they should adopt them, too. The foster Dad even told my parents that the Lord spoke to him and said, "Mike and Kris are supposed to adopt Matthew." (There is so much more to this testimony, but I'll leave that for my parents or Misty and Matthew themselves to share!)

So, with that being said they proceeded to get those two foster kids in our home and after some time they adopted them! I now had a sister; Misty Ann, who changed her name to Misty Maureen, and a brother; Matthew Allen, who changed his name to Matthew Michael at the time of adoption. I was 15, Misty was nine and Matthew was seven at their time of adoption. Shorty after their adoption, Misty and I had a double birthday party together because are birthdays are so close. We had a "Sweet 16 and Double Digits 10" for our joint birthday celebrations! Two big milestones in each of our lives! Around this time is when we left this church.

CHAPTER FOUR

"A NEW BEGINNING"

After this, my parents were led to a non-denominational church called, "Shekinah Worship Center" in Lancaster, California. I don't remember how it all happened, but my Mom and Dad felt led to leave Harvest church and start coming to Shekinah church. We went from a Baptist church in Palmdale to a non-denominational church in Lancaster! Kind of crazy, huh?! It was definitely different. Our Baptist church did believe in the spiritual gifts and speaking in tongues, but only the Pastor's wife practiced them. They never really taught that it was for the whole body. We always thought it was only for the leadership. We didn't know enough about it yet. This church, Shekinah, did believe in the gifts and taught that everyone could and should have them and use them. At this church we learned a lot about spiritual gifts, speaking in tongues, and the prophetic. It was exciting to see what else the Bible said beyond being "saved."

Oh, and just to tell you what happened at Harvest Church after we left; it closed down. Shortly after we left there arose problems within the leadership. I should say there already were problems within the leadership, but they finally came to a head and surfaced publicly. The church split and everyone went their separate ways and joined different churches. Some went to "The Vineyard" and some went to other churches around the valley. It was very sad because we were all so close and then we were all split up and pretty much lost that close bond. We still tried to keep in contact with the people from that church, but just about all of our friends from there were very upset at me and with my parents for leaving the church.

Before the Pastors made that announcement and before we left, my parents had a meeting with the Pastor to let him know they felt led by God to leave and go to Shekinah. My parents told our friends we were leaving, too. They were all angry and couldn't understand why we would leave. They insisted that once you are in a certain church body or congregation, that you don't leave. They said we are family and that we shouldn't leave to go to another church. When my parents explained how they didn't understand why, either, but they knew God was having them leave for a reason, they didn't get that. I guess maybe that's what they had been taught and didn't realize they were prioritizing loyalty to their church family over obedience to the Lord. They were upset and a lot of them stopped talking to my parents because they were offended that we left, but I am sure once they saw what happened after we left, they must have realized that God was really speaking to my parents.

God saved us from the hurt and heart ache of what we would have went through had we stayed. He prepared our hearts to leave and got us out of there before we experienced that devastation. I also believe He led us to a non-denominational church to teach us more things we would have never seen or been taught had we stayed at a Baptist church. That is not to say anything bad about the Baptist church, but they just don't teach a lot of what the New Testament says about the prophetic realm. They don't teach about Prophets and Apostles. They only teach three out of five of the five fold ministry purpose in Ephesians 4:11 KVJ, (And he gave some, apostles; and some, prophets; and some, evangelists; and some, pastors and teachers;). They teach about Pastors, Teachers, and Evangelists only, or at least at out specific church they did. Maybe it's not the case in every Baptist church, but it is what I experienced.

At this new church, Shekinah, on our first visit there, I went up for prayer. An older lady prayed for me and gave me a prophetic word, of which I had never had before. She told me that I was a gift all wrapped up and that God wanted to unwrap me and share me with others. I was His gift to be enjoyed by others. I had felt hurt from our friends being upset with us for leaving the other church, but this word gave me encouragement and I knew God had more for me to learn.

I joined the youth group at this church and went to Friday morning prayer meetings with my Mom. I helped serve one Saturday a month at our food outreach. I went to church with my parents on Sundays and on Thursday nights. I learned about the gift of tongues. One Sunday I went up for prayer because I wanted to be baptized "In the Spirit" and "with fire" like the Bible talked about. I was prayed for by our Pastor's wife and another gentlemen. After they prayed over me, I received the gift of tongues! I could now speak in tongues! I was "baptized in the Spirit!" They then taught me what that meant. I was learning all kinds of new things from the Bible that I hadn't grasped yet. Even though I had read about them and studied them over the previous years, because it was not taught or applied at our previous church, I never walked in them.

I was loving life and loving all the new truths I was learning. I was growing in the Lord, making new friends, and growing up physically and spiritually. At this time our church also opened a private Christian school called "Shekinah Christian School". It was only for Junior High and Senior High. I wanted to go to it. A few of my friends from church were going to enroll in it and I thought it would be fun to finish out High School with my friends at a Christian school. So, my parents prayed about it and took me off Independent Study and enrolled me in this school. I started going there for my eleventh grade school year.

CHAPTER FIVE

"A BOYFRIEND!?"

I was not really into wanting to date during this time. I had crushes on boys and all that, but I wanted my focus to be on Jesus. I knew He would bring the right one for me in His time. There had been several guys (three to be exact) that liked me over the years and all three of their Moms told me that I was the one that was supposed to marry their son. They would tell me that the Lord spoke to them and that I was to be their son's wife. Now, I'm not a genius, but if God told all three of them I was "the one", that would have been a problem! So, my conclusion was that God didn't tell any of them I was the one or maybe He told one of them and the other two were just hoping. One of them I kind of liked and I prayed about it and asked God if he was the one. I felt a lot of confusion and just finally gave it up and decided to wait before pursuing anything with him. Nothing came of it. I was now 16 and in my last year of High School. I know I told you I was in eleventh grade, but I also did twelfth grade the same year. So, yes, I was doing two grades at once. Even though it was my eleventh grade year, my "Junior year", it was also my "Senior year"!

I want to mention that also, at this same time, my parents were still doing foster care and they got a call to take in a new baby girl! They prayed about it and said, "Yes". I think she was just days old or maybe a couple of weeks old. We took her in as our foster sister/daughter. She was very sick and was in the hospital for a long time. She was premature from drugs and had pneumonia, among other things. The Doctors didn't even know if she would make it. With my Mom, me and our Pastor's wife at the hospital day after day praying for her and over her, she did make it! She survived and got to come home! There is a very long four-year testimony to what happened to her and to us during the first four years of her life, but I am not going to get into it. Let's just say that God is good and she is adopted now! So, I now had a second sister, Audrianna Jade Louise, which my parents shortened to just Audrianna Jade, who was only just a new baby when I was in my Senior year of High School! We are 17 years apart! I turned 17 right after she was born!

Now, it was in my Senior year in High School that I met my future husband. I was still going to Shekinah Glory Church. My future husband's parents started attending this church in September of 2000. This was at the beginning of my first and last year of High School at this church. The first time I saw my future husband he was sitting in a chair; slouching down, with his head leaned back on the chair. He had a hat on and it was really low so I couldn't even see his eyes. My friend Amanda said, "Hey, I know that kid! That's Mikey Martinez." I had known a boy named Mikey Martinez, so I first wondered if it was the same kid I knew, but it wasn't. I did think it was funny that they had the same first and last name though. I remember Amanda taking me over to where he was sitting to say hi and to "Meet the new kid in church." I said hi and introduced myself, and no, there was no "Love at first sight." I wasn't very impressed. Mikey seemed like he did not want to be there at church and he seemed like he had a bad attitude.

Time went by and he started coming to youth group on Thursday nights. He still didn't really seem interested to be there and kept somewhat to himself. The only other person he really knew was a neighbor of his, named Elijah, who was the Pastor's son. I remember he didn't ever want to come to youth group and he wouldn't ever come to events when we invited him because he would say he had a soccer game. A few more months went by and he enrolled in our High School as well. He enrolled half way through the school year, I believe around January of 2001. This was his Freshman year in High School. It was my Senior year. I was doing my 11th and 12th grade years together in one year so I could hurry up and be done with school! I didn't really like school anymore and I just wanted to be done with it and move on in my life. I didn't know how old Mikey was or what grade he was in at first because they had all the High School students in one, big class; 9th-12th all together. So, we figured we were about the same age.

At first I didn't talk to him much. He seemed into himself, a little on the perverted side, and very flirty with all the girls. That sort of behavior turned me off, so I didn't really go out of my way to make friends with him. After some time went by though I started getting to know him better since he was in my class and went to my church. I could start seeing that there was more to him than the typical egotistical guy thing going on. I could see he was hurting and just trying to find acceptance. I started being kind to him and would talk to him every now and then. At some point my disgust for him turned into compassion. I started praying for him. One day, at a morning prayer, Mikey's Mom was there. She said he had been hurt by his girlfriend because she cheated on him. I told her that I knew about it and that I had been praying for him. In fact, that night before I had been up till 3:00 a.m. praying for him. He was on my heart and I felt like God wanted me to pray for him. I told her that. She went home and told Mikey, "There is a really sweet girl at church that was up praying for you last night." His Mom liked me. When Mikey heard this he was so surprised that someone was actually thinking of him and cared about him enough to take time to pray for him. He was really touched by that.

Soon after that it seemed like he started taking an interest in me. I think he could tell there was something different about me. I wasn't like all the other girls he had liked or been with. I wasn't flirty. I didn't wear provocative clothes. I wasn't there to impress any guys. I was just real. Later, he told me that is in fact what attracted him to me and that he could see my love and passion for God and that he liked that. So, I was noticing that he started paying more attention to me. He would come to me and talk to me at my desk. He would play with my calculator (it was a really cool one that opened by itself)! I remember he would do crazy stuff to get my attention. For example: he would go to his locker, grab his "Happy For Men" cologne and spray it all over himself and then run by me! I remember he would do funny things like that to get my attention and make me laugh.

At this point is when I started liking him as well and taking an interest in him, too. I thought if he is trying so hard to get my attention, including making a fool of himself, he must really like me. I loved that he would make me laugh. I always wanted to be with a guy who could and would make me laugh. Even though he was giving me a lot of attention now, he was still very intimidated by me. He had heard about how "tough" I was and he had my friends telling him, "You better not get too close to her or try to kiss her or anything, or she'll punch you in the face." I wouldn't have punched him in the face, but I did make it clear that whoever I was going to be with was not going to be physical with me until we got married. So, he was very scared to ask me out or to even let me know that he liked me.

One day we took a field trip to the park with our class. Everyone was up on the hill doing something and Mikey went down to get a drink of water from the fountain, so I followed him. I was blunt with him and said, "Do you like me?" I said, "I hear rumors from your friends that you like me, but you won't tell me yourself. So, do you like me or not?" I didn't want to be lead on or fall for a guy who didn't really like me, so I wanted to know now before my emotions got too far into it. He looked pretty scared to answer me. He kind of hesitated for a minute and then said, "Yes, I do like you. Is that okay?" I just kind of laughed at him! He was so nervous to let me know that he liked me that he felt he had to ask my permission if it was okay that he liked me. (Poor guy!) So, that's why I laughed. I found it humorous. I guess I was playing hard to get or something because I didn't even tell him that I liked him, too! I just said, "Good. Yes, it's okay if you like me." Then I walked off and left him hanging, not telling him that I liked him, too.

Since that day, and since I knew he now liked me, I started letting my guard down more and became friends with him. We started hanging out more at school and flirting and all that stuff! He would draw me pictures and still run by me after spraying his cologne. The school year was coming to an end now and I was getting ready to graduate. Graduation day came and of course Mikey was there! He made me a home-made card with bright colors and daisies, just like I liked! After my graduation, we were all going to Marie Calendar's for pie to celebrate. I invited him and he came! I guess you could say this was our "first date", although my family and friends were there, too! It was the first time we actually went together anywhere. He drove with me in my new car that my Grandpa had just given me as my graduation gift! He seemed very nervous and wouldn't eat! LOL! We talked a little, but not much. I just remember being so happy that he liked me and came to celebrate with me.

Graduation Day! Me and Mikey! ~2001

So, now, of course, Summer was here! Even though we both had jobs and worked full time, we spent every free moment we had with each other. Well, let me back up a minute. After graduation, my Dad wanted to take me and some friends to Magic Mountain to celebrate me being out of High School! Mikey came, along with his best friend, Brandon, and my best friend, Amanda. We had a lot of fun! The four of us best friends and my Dad. Mikey had not yet "Asked me out", so I could tell he wanted to. The whole day I could tell he was waiting for the right moment, but he was so nervous, especially with my Dad being there! So, we just had fun and went on rides all day.

Finally, at night before leaving, we went on one last ride- "The Log Jammer"! My Dad went to get the car and was going to meet us up front. So, the four of us went to get in the log. Mikey and I stepped in and I waited and looked at my friend, but her and Brandon didn't get in. They waited there kind of giggling and smirking and got in the next log. So, I knew something was up. They had all probably planned it so Mikey could have his opportunity "alone" with me to ask me out! So, about halfway through the ride Mikey got up the nerve and nervously said, "Lacy, will you go out with me?" Now, for those of you older folks that don't know what that means, it means Mikey wanted me to be his official girlfriend and he wanted to start dating me. So, I said, "I would like to go out with you, but you have to change first." He said he knew that was coming and that's what he was afraid of. He knew I wanted to be with someone who was walking with the Lord and who was living his life in a holy manner, being set apart from the world. I explained to him what I meant. I said, "I like you, I really do, and I would love to go out with you, but I just can't right now with the way you are choosing to live." He knew I wasn't trying to make him feel bad and he already understood what I meant.

He wasn't really living for the Lord at this time. We were friends, but I knew the Scriptures about not being unequally yoked with an unbeliever as a Husband. He claimed and professed to be a "Christian", but his life didn't show fruit that he was one. He grew up believing he was a Christian. That's what his parents told him. He went to church. His parents were Christians and his Grandpa was a Pastor so he figured he was a Christian, too. That is not what makes someone a Christian though. I could see that he wanted to be a genuine Christian, but just didn't really know how to. No, I was not "judging" him in a wrong way and he didn't feel judged. It was just apparent that he was living for himself, not the Lord. His speech was sometimes perverted. He was into bad secular music, like Blink 182. He wasn't always truthful. Those things not only turned me off, but the Bible says to, "Not be unequally yoked," (see 2 Corinthians 6:14 NKJV). I knew that I had to obey the Bible, no matter how bad my flesh wanted to be with Mikey and be his girlfriend. I knew there had to be a real change that would occur in Mikey's heart before we could talk seriously about being together. To know if he was really a "Christian" and to know if he really was "saved" and living for the Lord, I would have to see that transformation and fruit in his life and I would have to see his love and commitment to God before I could really say, "Yes."

I know that was hard for him to hear, and hard for me to say, but it was the truth and it had to be said and heard. I knew if he really did like me and wanted to be with me, he would take what I said to heart and think about it. I also knew if he really loved me and knew me, he would not be offended by what I said, but digest it and be grateful that someone told him the truth about how he was living and how it wasn't pleasing to God. So, from that night, I just continued to pray for him. I really prayed. I prayed that he would really give his heart to the Lord and see how wonderful it is to lay down his own desires and trade them for the Lord's desires. I prayed he would surrender to God and give up the things that weren't pleasing to Him. Oh, I also prayed that if this was the Lord's will, for me to be with Mikey, that He would make it clear to me and give me the love and grace to help Mikey and to be patient waiting for him.

Chapter Six

"YES, A BOYFRIEND! COURTING, NOT DATING"

A couple of weeks went by and he called me one night. He said, "I've changed! I gave my life to God tonight! I broke and threw away all of my Blink 182 c.d.s and the other c.d.s I had that were bad. I ripped the Blink 182 posters off my wall and tore them up and threw them away! I cried, I repented, and I'm not going back to this way of living any more!" Of course, I lit up! I had a smile on my face from ear to ear! I was so excited for him (and for me)! I asked him, "What happened? What made you do that?" (I wanted to hear why he did that. Was it just for me? Did he do it just as a front so he could be with me now? Or did God work something in his heart?) He said, "My parents went to church tonight, but I didn't want to go. I asked them if I could stay home. After some begging, they said, "Okay". I was so tired of how I was living and how the enemy had me so oppressed. I was so sucked into this perverted music and tired of how it was making me feel. I finally decided that I am done with it. After my parents left, I put on a c.d. that you gave me. It was the band from New Zealand and I put on the song called, "Breakthrough." When I put that song on, something just changed inside of me. I had like a righteous anger and zeal stir up in me. I got mad at the devil and started yelling at him. Then, I cried and asked God for help and I asked Him to save me from the mess I am. He did! I feel so different now! The feeling of oppression left me and I feel like a new person!"

I was so happy to hear all of that, but there was still a small part of me that was telling me to be cautious. People can say the words, but their actions will show their heart. I wanted to start "dating" him immediately. I did believe what he said was true. I did believe he threw away his c.d.s and asked God for help. I remember I went out into the living room to tell my parents what had happened to Mikey. I told them what he had just told me over the phone. Darrell was there, too. (Darrell West, we truly miss you. Rest in peace.) Darrell was my Dad's best friend. He was over that night. I remember him and my Dad telling me to, "Wait and see." They said if this was really God and Mikey wasn't making it up, that time would tell and his actions would show if he was telling the truth. "Wait" is not what a young girl wants to hear! But I did. I waited patiently and sometimes didn't feel so patient! I saw him at church that next week and I did notice a change in him. I saw him at church and church events and he was "different" now. I could see it in his eyes. He start being more loving toward people; more self-less, instead of selfish. I could see a fire and desire for God start to burn and develop in him that I never saw before.

We finally talked and agreed to "Be together", but that also meant asking our parents for permission. That was the right thing to do since the Bible tells us to "Honor our parents." At this time, I was now 17 3/4 and Mikey was only 15 3/4. I was almost 18 and he was almost 16! I know that seems really young, and we were young, but we were mature for our age. We both had good jobs, we had our own cars that were completely paid off, we had no debt, we paid for our own car insurance, we were both now following God, etc. (Mikey wasn't quite 16 yet, so he didn't have his driver's license, but he did have his driver's permit.) So, we went nervously to each set of our parents and asked them if we could "Court" and officially be together. They both said that they wanted to talk to each other first to see what the other set of parents had to say. My parents wanted to talk to his parents and his parents wanted to talk to my parents. They wanted to talk and figure it all out together. That sounded good to us, so we got them together and they talked.

After they talked (and Mikey and I prayed that they would all say, "Yes"), they did say, "Yes" and decided we could "Court." I'm sure Mikey's parents had never heard of courting before. They used to just let Mikey "date" and go over to his girlfriend's houses, the movies, the mall, etc. My parents, on the other hand, were very strict and very protective over me. After all, I was the first born and I was a girl (lol), so they were very cautious about how to proceed with me and boys! My Dad had heard a thing from Dennis Rainey about "Courtship". "Courting" or "Courtship" basically means you date the girl/boy you like, but you also date their family, too. It is like group dating or family dating, not one on one. For example, Mikey would come over and eat dinner with me AND my family, instead of taking me on a date alone. And visa versa, I would go over there and eat dinner with him AND his family. This way we not only got to know each other, be we also got to know each other's family and not have the temptation to fall into sin from being alone.

Mikey and I were fine with this. As long as we could be together, we didn't care. And it wasn't as if I had much choice. It was either family dating or nothing. So, back to where I was, this is when we started hanging out a lot over the remainder of our Summer. We spent every free moment we could together (except when we had hang out times with our friends). I'd go to his house, he'd come to mine. Sometimes our parents would get together and we'd all hang out, etc. We got to know each other pretty well over the Summer. Mikey would come over and paint Scooby Doo on the wall in my room (I liked Scooby Doo back then and he's an artist!) and I'd go to his house and help his Mom put a desk together or help with cheerleading stuff (his Mom was a cheerleading coach). We loved being together. When we couldn't be together, we could call and text each other! You know, the joy of falling in love! We would read the Bible together and pray together in my parents 2nd living room while they would be watching t.v. in the 1st living room. We were never left alone, but both our parents gave us space to be together. We hung out with our friends, too; sometimes together, sometimes separate.

I had two good friends that would come over often and Mikey also had two good friends that he would go over to their houses to hang out. At this time, Mikey was also in a band with his brother and one of his best friends. They would have band practice together. Sometimes I would come and watch. Sometimes Mikey and my two friends, Kristal and Amanda, would come over to my house at the same time. We'd have fun, laugh, go swimming, etc. Then sometimes I would go to Mikey's house while his best friend and brother were there. We had a great first Summer "together"!

Eventually, the Summer came to an end and it was time for him to go back to school and I started college. It was a little weird because I had just graduated from High School at 17 and was now starting college, while my new boyfriend was going back to High School. He was only in 10th grade now and he was only 15 years old! We didn't care about our age difference. However, I didn't really like the fact that he was still in High School while I was in college. It felt kind of weird. Here, I was becoming more mature, out of High School, and moving on in my life. Yet, he was still in the High School drama and goofing-around scene. It was awkward at times, but we made it work! We just took one day at a time. Soon, after he started back in school, he turned 16, so it didn't seem like he was so young anymore. He decided he didn't want to be in High School for three more years, so he did three years of school in two years. He did what I did. He took all his 11th grade classes and 12th grade classes and combined them into one year, his Senior year. He now had two years left of High School, instead of three. At least two years was better than three years, but still, two years is a long time!

Those two years seemed to go by so slow, seeing as how we just wanted to be together and school was in the way. LOL! I filled my time with college. I went to a community college in Lancaster called "Antelope Valley College". I never had a desire to go to a "real" college, but I wanted to take some classes of my choosing at this community college. I took lots of dance classes, Sign Language classes, music classes, and vocal classes. I always loved to dance and sing and ever since I was little I have been fascinated with Sign Language. I wanted to learn it as a second language. I went to a dance class five days a week, along with my other classes. I was so skinny because I danced all the time, only 110 pounds! It was fun and I enjoyed all of my classes!

At this same time I also had a job at Lowe's. I had got a job at Lowe's from a friend of ours at church that was a Manager there. He hired me to work in the "Home Decor" section. I enjoyed it. I ordered blinds and curtains for people, helped them with wallpaper questions, and actually cut blinds for my customers. I worked there pretty much full time while I was in college. I had this job so I could pay for my own car insurance, gas, and food. My parents taught me responsibility at a young age and made me pay for my own things.

On my free time, I would still, of course, visit Mikey. I would try and bring him some lunch sometimes to school. He only went to school Monday through Wednesday and home schooled Thursday and Friday. That is how the school was set up through our church. I would see him whenever I could. I would drive to his house on my lunch breaks from work! I had an hour break every day and his house was 20 minutes away. I would drive through and get Taco Bell and drive to his house. I'd have 15 minutes to see him and then I'd have to drive 20 minutes back. You might say it was a waste of time, money, and gas, but not to me. Those 15 minutes I got to see him were worth it! Mikey also worked during this time. He worked with his sister at a tanning salon. No, it was not his choice to work there. His parents made him work there. He did not enjoy it. He hated the smell of burning flesh and having to clean all the smelly sweat off the beds when the girls were finished. Even though he didn't enjoy it, he worked there to have money to pay for his car insurance. I would go and visit him there sometimes, too, when it was slow and he would text me when he was bored.

Chapter Seven

"NO MORE BOYFRIEND?!
THE UNCONCEIVABLE SPLIT"

After two years of getting to know each other more, and getting to know each other's families more, it was finally time for Mikey to Graduate! So, in June 2003 he graduated High School. He was now 17 3/4 years old! He was almost 18, but not quite yet. In the Summer, after his graduation, he started attending the same college I was attending. He took a Summer class for computer graphics. He always liked graphics and animation and thought maybe he could learn it to be a graphic designer. During this time was one of our "hard" seasons. Let me explain. Mikey's parents had not grown very fond of me. They didn't like that I spent so much time with their son. They didn't like how much time he spent with me. They decided I wasn't "The right one for him." So, they took action and decided that Mikey could no longer see me. Even though we had been together for two years now and they said it was okay for us to court, they changed their minds and took measures into their own hands.

They told Mikey that he could no longer see me, ever again, and that he could no longer talk to me. They told me not to call him or text him anymore. His Dad even told me that if I called Mikey and talked to him that he would put a restraining order on me. They took things to the extreme, and very abruptly. You can imagine how I might have felt at this point. After hearing all that, I felt so many emotions. I don't even know where to begin. I guess you could say that my first feeling was rejection. I felt completely not liked, not wanted, and rejected by Mikey's family, and I didn't know why. I felt that they hated me and without a cause. I had always been kind to them and obeyed their rules for us and then this is how I was repaid by them? The next emotion I felt was anger. I was so angry at them for tearing me and Mikey apart. I was angry that they did it suddenly and without reason or explanation.

I was also heart-broken. It felt as if someone took my heart, threw it on the ground, and shattered it. I was sad. I was sad because I didn't have my best friend to hang out with anymore. I was devastated. I felt as if the relationship I had built with Mikey was gone now. I was confused. What did I do wrong? Why didn't they like me? Isn't this the person God has for me to be with? I didn't understand. With this flood of emotions overwhelming me, all I could do was burst into tears, fall to my knees with my face to the ground, and pray to God for help and vindication. I cried, I prayed, and I poured out my heart to God. I remember playing a song by Rebecca St. James called, "Hold Me Jesus." The words were, "Hold me, Jesus, I'm shaking like a leaf. You have been king of my glory, won't You be my prince of peace?" I remember crying as I sang that song over and over again to God, asking for Him to please come and be my peace and give me His peace through this difficult time.

Now, as I stated earlier, they asked me not even to see or talk to Mikey anymore. At this time I was now 19 1/2 years old, well past the age of "accountability" and well past the age of a "legal adult". I wasn't a kid anymore and I was not an immature teen. Mikey was now 17 1/2, almost an "adult". Of course I told my parents everything. I believe at some point they also called and talked to Mikey's Dad to see what the problem was. My parents did not agree or approve of what they were doing or the decision they made for me not to see or talk to Mikey again. They thought it was absurd. They felt if Mikey or/and I had done something wrong that we should discuss it all as adults and get it worked out. The way to solve problems is to communicate and talk things out, not to just go "cold turkey" and quit the relationship without any understanding of why. Mikey's parents were not willing to talk with me or my parents and they didn't want to talk anything out. I believe the reason why they didn't want to talk it out was because there was nothing to talk out. We hadn't done anything wrong, so they had nothing to accuse us of. I think deep inside, whether they realized it or not, they were hurting. I think they felt hurt that their son wanted to be with me more than he wanted to be with them. I think they were hurt by the fact that he could feel comfortable coming to me and talking about real life issues, but he didn't feel comfortable talking to them. He was their youngest son and the baby of the family. They didn't want to "lose" him to me.

My parents told me that they didn't agree with what his parents said. They said I was still aloud to see Mikey whenever I wanted. They said I was 19 and responsible enough to make my own decisions and to pray if this is who God wanted me to be with or not. They said if this was who God had for me, then I needed to pray, wait, and allow God to work. I did just that. I knew this is who God had for me, but the situation did cause me to doubt. "God, if this is who you have for me, then what is going on? Why can't I even see or be with this person I love?" This is one of the questions I had. Little did I know then that this was just another thing God wanted to take me (and Mikey) through to make us stronger. I know that what the enemy had used to try and separate us, God used for good. The enemy wanted to tear Mikey and I apart permanently, but by God's faithfulness, he didn't succeed. We just became stronger people and closer to each other through this time. By closer, I mean mentally and emotionally; not physically.

Now, I didn't talk to or see Mikey for a while because I was still trying to remain godly in this situation. I was still trying to show love for Mikey's parents, Mike and Tammy, by honoring what they asked. I also didn't want to make them even more mad. I complied for a while, as well as Mikey. I could only do that for so long. My heart ached to see him. Not only did I want to see him, but I was worried about him. I knew He was not as strong in the Lord as I was. He knew He wasn't that strong in the Lord yet, too. He had struggled with rejection and things before from his Dad and by me knowing how they were treating him during this time made me worry for him. I wanted to see him so bad just to make sure he was okay. I wanted to encourage him in the Lord and tell him to hang in there and that it would be okay in the end.

My Mom could see how bad I was hurting and how often I would go in my room and cry, as if grieving for someone who had passed away. I think she finally had enough of the non-sense and had enough of seeing me hurt. So, one day while out running errands with my Mom, she took me to Mikey's work so I could see him for a minute. I think we even brought him lunch. This was when he was working at the tanning salon called, "Bronze Buns". I mentioned earlier, he did not want to work there, but his parents made him work there so they could "keep an eye on him." Mikey's sister had worked there and they also knew the owner. So, whether it was Mikey's sister or the owner, they could tell on Mikey if he saw me or talked to me. Anyway, I remember the day we saw him. He was so happy to see us! He was also very distraught. I could see in his eyes and face how bad he was hurting. I could see the discouragement in his eyes; the confusion, the hurt, the unbelief that this was really happening. Everything I was feeling, he was feeling. We were both just trying to figure it all out and we were trying to make sense of everything.

There was another time I saw him. I was at college and on my way to my dance class. Mikey was there at the same time for his computer graphics class. He came out to see me and I saw him there and met him outside with open arms. We both hugged and cried, told each other to hang in there and then went back to class. I'm sure Mikey's Dad was there in the parking lot spying on Mikey to make sure he didn't see me (cause he knew we both had classes on Saturday). I know he was there because he had mentioned it at a later time that he saw me with Mikey at school together. I guess I will never know exactly what really happened, but I assume because of Mike seeing me hugging Mikey that day and because of me seeing Mikey at work the other time, Mikey's parents must have went to our Pastors to discuss our "disobedience."

Mike and Tammy went to our Pastors and accused us of being "rebellious teenagers" who didn't listen to them and didn't honor them. I guess they went to gossip about us and to get our Pastors thinking bad about me and Mikey and to get them on their side. Knowing my parents didn't agree with what they were doing, I think they were trying to get someone to be on their side. So, that's what ended up happening. They got our Pastors on their side and convinced them that we were just bad, rebellious kids. They said we were selfish and not following God, which was far from the truth. I guess Mikey's parents had searched Mikey's room for anything they could find to use against us. They succeeded.

They found some letters that I had written to Mikey. I loved to write. I wrote all the time. I was taking English classes in college and getting A's and it was my best and favorite subject. So, I wrote all the time, including to Mikey. I didn't just write letters to him, but also to my friends, family, sponsor child, etc. I was always writing. In my letters to Mikey, I would encourage him to follow the Lord, I wrote Scripture verses, told him how much I loved him, talk about upcoming events, and stuff like that. In at least one of my letters I had wrote for him to pray for his parents. I told him to pray for them to hear and listen to God and to pray for them to be obedient to God's word and for them to realize what they were doing. I don't believe they even understood the depths of how bad they hurt us by what they were doing. I was hoping they would eventually see that and realize the pain they were causing us.

Side note: This is worth mentioning right now because it was a part of what they read in one of my letters. Mikey's parents also forced him to stay in his band even though he no longer wanted to be in. This was the band I mentioned earlier with his brother and best friend. He enjoyed it for a while and fun playing. His brother had arranged for them to start playing at bars and clubs and it started really convicting Mikey. He started not to like it and felt uneasy in his spirit to be playing in those places where drinking and smoking was prevalent. When he had told his parents this conviction and told them that he wanted to quit the band and not be yoked with it anymore they wouldn't let him quit. They said he had a calling to play with his brother and would not allow him to quit. They were his parents and he wasn't 18 yet, so they had him stay in it. I believe they thought it was me and my persuasion to get him to quit, when, in reality, it was him. Of course I didn't like it. I didn't want him playing secular music at bars and clubs, either, but it was his decision. They forced him to stay in it and play at the clubs and bars anyway. I guess they didn't think it was wrong. I had wrote to Mikey to pray for them to seek God in this matter. Mikey and I were honestly hoping that they would be convicted by God for making him play at those venues. I had written in the letter for Mikey to pray for his parents so that they might finally let him leave the band that he so badly wanted to get out of.

Because of that letter, and other letters in general that I wrote to Mikey, they didn't like it. They didn't like me writing him letters. So, Mikey's Dad, Mike, told me I could no longer write to Mikey, either. They brought the letters to the Pastors (by Pastors I mean our Pastor and his wife) to talk about me and to make a case against me. They convinced themselves that because I wrote that about them hearing and listening God in the letter(s) that I was disrespectful, rebellious, and controlling, among other things. Those were the top three that I was told. Therefore, they told the Pastors that this is why they didn't want Mikey to be with me. They said I was disrespectful and didn't honor their decisions. Even though there was a hint of truth in their accusations against me; like the fact that I didn't agree with their decisions, not once did they try to talk to me about it. Instead, they just chose to accuse me, hate me, reject me, go behind my back to the Pastors, and then not allow me to court their son anymore.

I want to add something else very awful, but also wonderful right here before I go on. After that meeting that Mikey's parents had with the Pastor, Mikey struggled with thoughts of suicide. Mikey was in that meeting with his parents and the Pastor. Both the Pastor and his parents accused Mikey of being rebellious and made him feel so little and literally like he was a piece of crap worth nothing of value, that he left that meeting telling himself, "If this is how "life" is and if this is how "Christians" are treating me; like I am nothing, then I am just going to go kill myself." He didn't feel like he was worth anything to them or to God. He didn't want to live anymore with all the hurt and pain he was feeling. He felt buried beneath condemnation and couldn't seem to get out.

He was planning to take his life that night, but while sitting in a chair, hunched down, in the church- waiting for the service to end so he could go home and end his life, a lady came up to him with hope. A lady at the church had received a word from the Lord for Mikey! She came over to him and hugged his neck from behind and then she looked at him and said, "Don't do it!" She continued to "read his mail" as the charismatics say (lol) and tell him everything he was just thinking in his mind. She said, "Don't let what you are going through right now cause you to end your life. God loves you and He has a plan for your life." She continued to love on him and encourage him as he sat there balling. He realized at that moment that God really did love him, even if no one else did. (He knew I loved him, but knowing that he couldn't see me anymore, he felt he had no hope and no one to help him now.) That changed him and he chose not to end his life. Isn't that awesome?! Isn't God awesome?! If it wasn't for God giving that lady that word for Mikey, and for her being obedient to give Mikey that word, Mikey might not even be here today. The devil and people's condemnation could have caused him to end his life early. Thank you God for keeping Mikey alive and thank you, Risa, for your love for Mikey to deliver that word to him and save his life!

You know, God sees you, right now, too- right where you are at. He loves you. He sent His son to die for you so that He can have a relationship with you and so He can give you His love. If you are reading this right now and are or have struggled with thoughts of suicide, don't so it. Know that God loves you! Ask Him to deliver you from those thoughts and to give you His hope and love for your life.

They were right in saying I didn't honor all their decisions. It probably wasn't my place to go against their decisions. I didn't know how to only trust God back then. I thought I had to convince people that what they were doing was wrong and get in the middle of it. I had such a passion for God and His righteousness, that the fact that another Christian didn't feel the same way as I did, I didn't understand. Not that I didn't honor them, I just didn't agree with them forcing their almost adult son to be in a "Christian" band while at the same time being yoked with the world, against God's will. They said I was rebellious for writing to him. I was never told not to write to him before that time. I was told I couldn't talk to him (like on the phone) and couldn't see him. So, I chose to write him during that time. They thought I was controlling for admonishing him to pray for them. They didn't think we needed to pray for them because they were convinced they were right.

CHAPTER EIGHT

"WE KEPT FIGHTING FOR US"

By taking the letters to the Pastors and convincing them that Mikey and I were rebellious caused even more problems. That brought our Pastors to side with Mikey's parents and be against my parents because they didn't all agree. It made our Pastor and his wife have a terrible outlook and view on who Mikey and I really were. I remember one night after that "meeting" the Pastors had with Mikey's parents I was leaving college and I had to meet the Pastor's wife in the parking lot on the way out to drop my sister off to her. She was going to go spend the night with the Pastor's daughter. I said hi to the Pastor's wife, was cordial, and she immediately started chewing me out.

She told me that I better, "knock it off" and stop being rebellious. She told me basically to just move on and not even try to see Mikey again. She told me that if I kept seeing Mikey or talked to him again that Mike and Tammy said they were going to take Mikey away and move to Huntington Beach, so that he was far enough away that I couldn't see him. She said I was on thin ice and that I better watch it! She said they would move him away from me and that they wouldn't tell me the address so that I couldn't find him and never see him again. I couldn't believe what I was hearing. You can imagine that didn't help me feel any better or give me any hope or encouragement.

I think I tried to explain to her that we weren't being rebellious or willfully doing anything wrong and that if they would do that, that they would just be pushing Mikey further away from themselves and that in a few months when he turned 18 he would leave Huntington Beach and come find me. I wasn't being sarcastic or arrogant by saying that. I just knew Mikey and I knew if they did that to him he would put a wall up in his heart against his parents and be hard-hearted toward them. When he turned 18 he would be ready to leave them and if they had pushed him away, they would be the ones not seeing him again. I said all of this while holding back tears. I knew he would leave them and not look back. He had already felt rejection from them and misunderstood by them and I knew if they moved him that it would make it worse. I think I told her that they better be careful by doing that so they don't push him away and lose him. She didn't like me saying that and basically kept chewing me out until I left balling, feeling beaten up and discouraged.

Driving home, feeling helpless and not knowing who to call or who to turn to, I was crying uncontrollably. I asked God what to do. I felt like giving up and just crawling up in a ball and hiding from life. I felt that no one understood me or understood the pain I was going through. I felt that the people putting me through this didn't know or want to know the pain I was going through. I knew in my heart and mind that I had lived a life to please God. I was being obedient, staying abstinent, reading my Bible, praying for God's will in my life, etc. What had I done so wrong to be treated like this by my own Pastors and by my boyfriend's family? I thought, "Is this how life is? Is this how Christians really are?" Well, I hated it! I wanted to call Mikey's Mom that night and ask her why they hated me and what I had done to them for them to hurt me so bad. I cried all the way home so angry and so upset and mad at the devil.

I believe I called my Dad and he didn't even know what to really say to me except to hang in there. I felt desperate to hear God and to know what was going on and I wanted the extreme pain that I was feeling to stop and go away so bad. With no where to go at this point, and with no one to turn to, I had to trust God. I had to trust Him to heal me, to restore mine and Mikey's relationship, to bring justice to what was wrongly being done to us, and to make things right. I didn't understand it all then, and I still don't understand it all fully now, but I do know that God allowed all of this for a reason. Looking back and thinking through everything in order to write this book is very painful. As I am remembering and recalling the events that happened over 10 years ago it is stirring up those emotions in me and bringing tears to my eyes as I am typing this. I was such a helpless, young lady who was so hurt, but God used it to make me stronger and to teach me how to trust in Him completely when people fail me and let me down.

So, now, as I got home, I cried and prayed in my room until I fell asleep. I had prayed for God's will to be done and for Him to help me and Mikey to be strong. I prayed He would teach us what we needed to learn and soften Mike and Tammy's hearts. I prayed that they would see what they were doing and how they were pushing Mikey further away. They thought that during this time of him not seeing me that they could spend more time with him and make up for all the years they hadn't been there for him. They started being home with him more, taking him to the movies, buying him clothes and shoes and trying to win him back to themselves, but he was very unhappy. Mikey later told me that his Dad would say things like, "Just forget about her. Be happy. Wipe that sad look off your face. Etc." His Mom would tell him, "There's plenty of other girls out there." They were realizing that he would be 18 soon and I think they were hoping he would just forget about me and stay with them longer. They didn't understand how deep of a bond Mikey and I already had and how much we really loved each other. It wasn't teenage lust. We needed each other and God planned for us to be together!

Mikey told me later that he would try to act happy around them, so he wouldn't get in more trouble and to not make his Dad angry, but he wasn't happy at all. He missed me and he missed being with me. His Mom would ask him, "What's wrong? Why are you so sad and why aren't you yourself?" He would tell her, "Because I miss Lacy and I want to be with her. I know that's who God has for me. She really loves me with a real love and cares for me and understands me." Finally, after such a long time of seeing this, I think his Mom started to realize that Mikey really did love me and miss me. I think she realized they were pushing Mikey away. I think she realized how unhappy he was and she was tired of seeing her son upset and not happy like he usually was. She could see what they had done wasn't working and that he wasn't getting "over me" like they hoped he would.

I believe now looking back that it wasn't something they necessarily had against me personally. They were just trying to control him so they wouldn't lose him. So, they grabbed the reigns and went to the extreme keeping him away from me. They were hoping our relationship would end, he would forget about me, and that he would live with them longer. Mikey was the "baby" of the family and they didn't want to let go of him. They wanted to keep him under their thumb and control his life so he didn't make the mistakes that his older siblings had made. That is understandable, but we all have to "let go and let God" at some point and not make the decisions for our children that they need to make for themselves. They had later shared all this with us, sort of, but that didn't make it any less painful when it was happening.

Chapter Nine

"A BREAKTHROUGH!"

So, months later, Mikey's Mom started intervening and asking his Dad if Mikey could slowly maybe start seeing me again. She said, "Just as friends, once in a while." Mike was not wanting that, but I think because of the hurt Tammy was finally starting to feel for her son and knowing Mikey was unhappy with his Dad, they said he could see me one day! Now, they think this was in their control and it was their decision, but I know it was God. God gets the glory for making things right! He is the one that moved on their hearts and caused them to have compassion for their son. He is the one that accomplishes His will at the end of the day. Mikey and I were praying and He was hearing our prayers. I felt so relieved the day Mikey called and said I could come see him, but at the same time I was hesitant and still very cautious to let my guard down.

During this time, I didn't give up. I felt helpless, discouraged, lonely, etc., yes, but I kept trusting God and hung in there. I went to a worship night type of thing in Lancaster one night. A prophet named Clyde Rivers was there. We were all worshipping for a while. I was worshipping, although I had this huge burden and oppression from the enemy weighing me down, I was still praising God. Clyde came up to me and said, (I'm paraphrasing because I don't remember exactly word for word) "Lacy, the Lord sees what you are going through. He is going to take care of it. He says He will make your enemies your footstool. Keep waiting on Him to do it and keep trusting Him." There was more to it, but that was the main point. God saw what the enemy was trying to do to me and Mikey, and by enemy I mean satan. Mike and Tammy were not my enemies, although it felt like it at times. The devil is our enemy. He just uses people to distort God's will and to try and tear people apart and get them to give up and quit. Thank God that He is God and the enemy can't stand against Him!

So, after that Mikey and I started hanging out again, but mostly at my house now. We didn't do much with his family after this, as you can imagine why. They didn't really want me around. Mikey and I kept praying together, reading the Bible, doing devotionals together, etc. We would talk about God and the things he has done with my family. Mikey learned a lot about God and what He can do through this time. He had never really seen any Christians truly live a life for God with answered prayers and prophetic words actually coming to pass. He was so grateful for my parents. By now, even after enduring separation (not by choice) for what seemed like years, we knew God had placed us together and we wanted to get married. We started talking about it more and praying about it. One day while we were at the mall we looked at the outside shelf of a jewelry store for engagement rings. I saw a ring that caught my eye instantly. It wasn't the typical ring that I saw on most girls with the band and one big diamond. It was very different. It was a unique heart ring. It had one big heart in the middle with a diamond in it and four smaller hearts on the sides, two on each side. I think I even tried it on. Mikey wanted to buy it for me right then, but we didn't have enough money and we wanted to pray about it first.

The ring was a $500.00 ring, but it had gone on a major clearance for like 75% off. It was now only $125.00. Even though it was super cheap, Mikey didn't have it. The money we made went toward gas in our cars, car insurance, and buying our own "eating out" food. We left and went to my house. We prayed again, "Lord, if this is Your will for us to get married and if this is the ring I am supposed to have, then provide the money for it." I'm sure I must have prayed on my own that night, too, that if this was the ring God wanted me to have, that Mikcy would have the money to buy it. Mikey said he had prayed that night, too, alone in his room at home, "Lord, if this is the ring I am supposed to get for Lacy, please provide me with the money for the ring."

He looked in his wallet before going to bed and it was completely empty. So, he thought maybe one day I'll have enough to get it for her. He went to sleep that night and had a dream that the money was being put in his wallet. So, the next morning he remembered the dream. So, with expectation, he grabbed his wallet from his dresser, right where he had left it, opened it, and ALL of the money for the ring was in there! There was more than the $125.00 in his wallet. God knew how much it would be including tax and the cost of sizing it. When Mikey later went to the mall to buy it, it was exactly enough! God is amazing, isn't He?! He is our provider and showed us that He was our provider at a young age, even before we were married. To those of you skeptics out there, I know what you are thinking. No, his parents didn't put the money in there. He asked them if they put any money in his wallet and they said no. They didn't even know about the ring. It was God!

He came to college that day and told me what happened and showed me the money! Not only was it the right amount, but they were like new bills laid out in order; a hundred, then a fifty, and some ones. We were both so excited and knew without a doubt that this was another confirmation from God that He meant for us to be together. Later, Mikey went and bought the ring, but hid it from me in his room until he knew from God when it was the right time to propose to me. He wanted to pray about it and ask for God's timing to officially propose to me. We already knew we would get married, but wanted to be careful about when to make it official. He wasn't quite 18 yet and wanted to be mindful of his parents and what they thought at this time, too.

So, I think it was a couple months that had gone by and it was our "when we started courting anniversary" and I asked Mikey, "So are you going to propose to me today?" He said, "No," and I was disappointed, but I knew he was waiting for the right time, even though I was impatient! We went iceskating in Valencia to celebrate our courting anniversary. It was very fun. This was at the end of June. Now, in July, I was going to go on a Mission trip with a prophet and a ministry team from our church. I had already raised the money to go and planned it during the time when Mikey and I couldn't be together. I figured it was something I could do for the Lord and also keep me busy while I wasn't able to see Mikey. The same week I was going to be gone on the mission trip happened to be the same week that Mikey's parents had planned a work trip or vacation or something of their own. Mikey couldn't go and they needed somewhere for Mikey to stay. My parents asked if Mikey could stay at our house while they were gone and explained to them how I wouldn't be there anyway because I would be in Mexico. Surprisingly, they said, "Yes" and let him stay with my family while I was gone.

I was going to be gone for 10 days and his parents were going to be gone for 14 days. They dropped him off the day before I had to leave. That night I was excited to go, but didn't want to leave him and my family. Mikey and I took a walk around our neighborhood and talked about the trip and he prayed for me. When we got back to my house, we went out back in our gazebo and he knelt down, asked me to marry him, and gave me the ring! He must have already told my parents because they were at the back watching and waiting for me to come in. Of course I said, "Yes"! The ministry team had told us not to wear or bring jewelry on the trip, so Mikey wanted to keep my ring with him. I came inside and my parents were like, "So, what did you say?" I told them, "I said, Yes, of course," as I was embarrassed.

The next morning they drove me to the airport and dropped me off. I was sad leaving and scared because I had never been on an airplane before. I saw one of my guy friends on the back of the plane, but I couldn't sit by him. All the seats were taken, except for mine in the middle by the window. We took off and landed in Houston, Texas and then from Houston we flew to Monterrey, Mexico. We flew into a hurricane! That was really scary, especially for it being my first time flying, but God kept us safe. This trip is a whole other testimony in and of itself so I'm not going to get into it right now. I will just say that it was a very scary, lonely, a little confusing, and long trip, but I was really close to God during those 10 days. I trusted him and saw miracles and people healed right before my eyes!

CHAPTER TEN

"THE ENGAGEMENT!"

At the end of this trip, I flew in to Ontario, California; exhausted and happy to be home! I was sitting at the very back of the plane (not by choice), which I'm sure God had set up. Needless to say, I was the very last person off the plane, anxiously waiting to get off of it and see Mikey and my family. I got off and made my way to luggage. As I was coming down the escalator, I noticed a huge crowd of people at the bottom. I wondered what was going on. Then I noticed they were forming a large circle at the end of the escalator where I was getting off. Then I saw why there was such a commotion! Mikey was kneeling there at the bottom of the escalator with the ring in his hand. My Dad had a video recorder in his hand. My brother was holding a big sign over Mikey's head that read, "Will you marry me, Lacy Megan?" Check "Yes" or "No". You know when you are kids and you send little letters around to the people you have crushes on saying, "Do you like me?" Check the box, "Yes" or "No." He was being funny and wrote it like that. He had a big "Yes" with a box next to it and a tiny "No" box next to it. My sisters and Mom were holding flowers, candy, and balloons from him to me.

I was slightly embarrassed, but surprised and happy! I said, "Yes" and gave Mikey a big hug and everyone in the airport clapped and the airport announcer guy over the radio said, "She said yes!" It was so very cool and funny! That was Mikey's plan. He wanted to keep the ring and give me an official, one-of-a-kind special proposal. I loved it! So, after this time we started praying about when God wanted us to get married. Mikey and I don't take anything lightly. We pray about everything. We asked God which date He wanted us to get married on. We didn't want to do our own will and what we wanted. We wanted to be in His perfect will. If it was up to us, we would have gotten married right away. We just wanted to be together so bad, without having to worry about restriction and control from Mikey's parents, but nonetheless, we would wait for God's timing. This was in July of 2003.

While praying about it, I felt in my spirit like God was saying "January 1st". I didn't think of that. I was thinking of having a Fall wedding or in June on the Anniversary day of when we started courting. I really felt impressed in my heart like the Lord was telling me, "The date I have for you and Mikey to get married is January 1st, New Years of this next year, 2004." So, I was like okay and I waited to see what Mikey would tell me. Mikey had prayed about it, too, and I didn't tell him the date I felt the Lord gave me. One day we were at college in the parking lot (I think Mikey was dropping me off for class) and we were just talking about what God was doing in our lives and I asked him if he had heard a date from the Lord yet. He said that when he had prayed about it and asked God when the date should be, that he literally saw the letters of the word "January" and the number "1" in front of his face! His eyes were shut when he prayed, but he saw "January 1st" go across his eyes in white letters from left to right as if he was reading it in front of him. So, when Mikey told me this, I got a big smile (of course) because I knew this was God and it was another confirmation that I was hearing God right and that we were on the right path and that He did want us to be together. I told Mikey what I heard God tell me and how it was the same date and we were both very excited. This was in August. Mikey was graduated, out of school and in college now and was working full time, but was still not 18. He wouldn't turn 18 until October. Two more months!

CHAPTER ELEVEN

"MORE CONFLICT"

So, what did this mean for us? We knew we were supposed to be together. We knew how God provided a ring for me. We knew how he worked it out for us to be together again and for Mike and Tammy not to move away. We knew how He showed us even the date of when our wedding would be. We were happy and excited. We shared this with Mikey's parents; about the ring and the date and that we were planning on getting married when we felt God was directing us to get married. That's when we both got an anvil dropped on our heads and more conflict broke out! They were angry, mad, furious, etc. They told Mikey, "No way. You're not getting married that soon. You are too young. You will never make it. You won't have enough money. Why are you rushing to get married? Is Lacy pregnant?" Yep, we heard all kinds of negative things bursting forth from their mouths and accusations started coming straight from the enemy through them. We were crushed... once again. They did not believe a word we said. They did not believe that we really prayed and that we could really hear from God. Mikey said they weren't used to that and it wasn't normal for them to hear God, so they didn't believe we could hear God, either.

They told us we were too young and told Mikey again to slow down and that there were plenty of other girls he could be with and not to rush into anything with me. They took Mikey to our Pastor without me and the Pastor told him basically the same thing. He told him that he was just a rebellious teenager. He was in agreement with Mike and Tammy, without knowing the truth of everything God had shown us and what had happened. Mikey's parents realized Mikey would soon be 18 and they would no longer have a say in what he did, so with two months left, they begged us to please separate ourselves from each other again for a while to pray about it separately. They wanted us to be apart again and to pray and think about it and make sure that God really wanted us to be together and be married. So, humbly and grudgingly submitting to them, we did just that. This was another painful season of two months being apart again. We sought God, asked him to confirm and show us if we really were supposed to be together and if not, to show us we were wrong and to help us break up from each other for good.

During this time, my parents started wondering about it, too. I don't think they wanted me to get married so soon in January, either. My Mom seemed like she was doubting that Mikey and I were supposed to be together. She would say things like, "Are you sure God told you this is the one?" "Are you sure you don't want to wait and make sure if there is someone else out there for you?" She would ask me questions like that and it would make me doubt that I was hearing God right. My Dad just was kind of like whatever about it. He would always say, "I support your decision, whatever you choose to do," but he also doubted that we would get married on January 1st. I remember one night through this time they reminded me of the story of Abraham with Isaac and they told me to lay Mikey on the altar and to leave him there. They said, "Leave him on the altar and don't take him back again. Then pray and if it is God's will then He will give Mikey back to you at the right time and you guys will be together." So, I did that. I said, "God, Mikey is Yours. If he is the one for me, then You work this out again and give him back to me and if not, then I lay him on the altar and You do what Your will is for his life." I know with all the things God had already showed us it would seem obvious that we were to be together, but you know how the enemy works. He caused us to doubt. I trusted God though, that He would make everything right.

This time was still very hard and difficult to go through, but I knew this was more of mine and Mikey's decision this time to separate ourselves so we could really focus on God and what He wanted for us. It was hard, but not as hard as the first time. I had loved the Lord since I was saved, and even before that, and I did want to make sure this was Him, for sure! Getting married is the biggest commitment you can make in life, besides choosing to follow Jesus, so I didn't want to take it lightly. So, after some time, we felt the Lord confirm to each of us that this was Him putting us together and again Mikey's parents could see Mikey missed me and longed to be with me. His birthday was approaching and they finally said he could see me again if he knew for sure that he was supposed to be with me. I think I finally saw him again on his birthday at their house. Tammy was finally okay with the fact that we were engaged and told me to call Mike "Dad" now. So, I went outside and said hi to him and called him "Dad," but it was really weird and awkward.

Now, Mikey had turned 18 and I turning 20 just 13 days later. Mikey started looking for a house for us. He wanted to get us a place and live in it alone for the months of November and December before we got married so he could learn how to take care of himself and pay the bills before I moved in. He found and moved into a two bedroom mobile home that an older couple at our church owned. He moved in toward the end of November. Mikey shared with his parents our plans and how he was getting his own place. They said okay and were fine with his plans, but when we started moving Mikey's stuff out, Mike was not okay with him moving out. He was upset at us.

Mikey still moved into the mobile home that day, but his Dad was mad and went to the Pastor again. A few weeks later, when Mikey came back home to get more of his things, his parents took him back to the Pastor and Mikey's Mom told him that he could be on his own and live in the mobile home, but not to marry me. They told him they wanted him to wait until June and then see if by then he still wanted to marry me. He was like, "What? Are you serious?" The Pastor told Mikey that even though he was now 18 he still needed to obey what his parents asked. So, Mikey told me what they said and we, wanting to obey God's word and honor his parents because we love God said, "Okay, we will wait until June and put off the wedding and not get married on January 1st." This is when I got confused though. I knew the date that God showed us. I thought about it and told Mikey, "Aren't we supposed to obey God, rather than men?" If we obey your parents and wait until June then we will miss God's will and timing, but if we obey God we will seem rebellious and disobedient to your parents and our Pastor.

We always tried to be a good, Christian example to everyone. Mikey and my parents said to just pray and if January 1st was still God's will then it will still happen and that He would honor us for submitting to Mikey's parents. We also didn't see why they wanted us to wait till June when that was just leaving more time for the enemy to tempt us from being pure. We had remained pure with each other and not had sex with each other. We thought; we know we are to be together, so why wait now that we know it is God's will? Let's get married so there is no room for the enemy to come in. Mikey's parents (and I believe even his extended family) accused me of being pregnant anyway and thought we weren't remaining pure. They thought that is why we were "rushing" to get married on January 1st.

Again, we said, "Okay, we will wait till June," but we kept praying for God's will and asked for His help with the situation. Mikey continued to live in the mobile home alone and I still lived at home with my parents. December rolled around and Tammy needed help at the clothing company she worked at. She needed "Christmas help." I went and worked with her for a few days, part time. It was in a city that was about an hour away, so we had an hour each way to talk. One day she asked me if I really wanted to marry Mikey. I said, "Yes." She was asking me a series of questions about him and if we really felt we were supposed to get married on January 1st. I answered them and said, "Yes." She said, "Well, okay then, I'll go home and talk to Mike about it." So, Mikey and I prayed and she went home and talked to Mike. The next day she told Mikey, "Okay, Dad and I decided it is okay for you get married on the first." We thanked God and gave Him the glory. The funny thing is that they think they were the ones in control of our wedding date and that this was their decision, but it was God who already ordained it before time. He orchestrated the whole thing and worked out what He had to work out in their hearts. The Bible says, "God turns the hearts of Kings..." so surely He could turn their hearts. This is why we can never get frustrated or impatient- because everything in life is just a test. It is a test that God uses to test our hearts and character. Will we trust Him no matter what we see and hear in front of us with our natural eyes and ears or will we complain and bicker- showing signs of disbelief? What the devil plans for evil and destruction, God turns into good for us and for His will!

CHAPTER TWELVE

"THE WEDDING... FINALLY!"

So, now with only two weeks left until January 1st, we had to plan a whole wedding! I had already still been planning for January 1st in my mind because I had faith that God would work it out for the day He said. We had already got the bridesmaid's dresses and some other things. My parents didn't have a lot of extra money then, but they did have enough to buy me my wedding dress and some decorations and Mikey's parents offered to pay for the rehearsal dinner. The Lord had tons of favor on us. The bridesmaids dresses were, I believe, $156.00, and they were on clearance for just $56.00- $100.00 off! My dress was on sale. Someone in our church offered to make our wedding cake for us for free! Someone in our church offered to d.j. for us for free! Mikey asked his Grandpa to do the ceremony and marry us because his Grandpa was a Pastor, and he was honored to do it... for free! We were going to have an outside wedding, but we couldn't find an outdoor place that we could afford. And with it being Winter, we figured it might be too cold and windy anyway. Where we lived it was a very windy desert, so we just decided to have it inside our church. Our Pastor's wife (by then must have had a change of heart about us) said we could have the wedding and reception at the church for free! Mikey's cousin was taking photography classes in college and offered to do our pictures for free as her wedding gift! My uncle video taped our wedding for free! I think we only spent about $300.00 on our whole wedding for the decorations, fake flowers, and other miscellaneous items (like our ring bearer pillows).

My Mom helped me make wedding invitations on our computer at home. I loved Cinderella back then, so we rolled the invitations up like scrolls and tied them with a ribbon, like in the movie. The ones we had to mail, we still rolled them and stuck them in an envelope. It was fun, creative and cheap! We also were able to pull off a bridal shower one week before the wedding. We hand wrote invitations for that and gave them out on that Sunday at church for that following Thursday. A week later, after the bridal shower, was our wedding on Thursday, January 1st, 2004. It seemed pretty rushed, but fun. We decorated the reception area with pink for me and black for Mikey. Those were our favorite colors at the time. The bridesmaids dresses were pink and the guy's suits were black. We did a Cinderella Princess theme with white and silver carriages on the tables and glass slippers.

As for our actual wedding ceremony, we wanted it to completely honor God. We didn't want to do the typical "American" wedding. By that I mean start a half hour late, have the Pastor read a pre-written vow paper, say vows, kiss, and then party. We wanted it to be different and lead by the Holy Spirit. We gave Mikey's Grandpa permission to do our wedding, of course, but also to say whatever else he felt lead to say. We told him to follow the Lord's leading to preach Jesus or whatever he felt led to do! He was a believing Christian, by the way, so he was all for that. Mikey and I also have a favorite Scripture together and it is Ephesians 2:22 NKJV which says, "In whom you also are being built together for a dwelling place of God in the Spirit." This is what Mikey and I wanted in and for our marriage. We wanted to be built together in Him so that He would dwell in the midst of our marriage and in our home physically. We wanted our marriage and home to honor and host Him, so we set our wedding time for 2:22 p.m. as a symbol that we would make that Scripture a reality in our lives! It was also a way for us to share with my unsaved family about that verse because they asked, "Why 2:22?"

The big day finally arrived! Nervous, excited, and happy- we were just glad it was finally here! There had been some people on Mikey's side of the family that were negative and told us no one would come because it was a holiday and because it was too late of a notice and that sort of thing, but we didn't care. We knew whoever really loved us would come and whoever was supposed to be there would be there. Sure enough- we were so blessed! All of my family came, most of our friends came (except a few that had to work), and most of our church family came. We were blessed with so many gifts and tons of money! God's favor was just all over the wedding and on us!

We weren't blessed just because of the gifts or the money, but because God's presence was there! We started the wedding promptly at 2:22 in the afternoon. When we all got up on the stage and were going to start, the Holy Spirit moved on Mikey's Grandpa and he started the ceremony by lovingly rebuking the people there. He said, "We are here to support Mikey and Lacy and their marriage. You all that have come here speaking negative words about them, you need to shut your mouth or leave! If you are speaking word curses over them and grumbling about them being too young or saying they won't make it, just stop. We have come today to be here for them and support them." It was so awesome. God had used him to rebuke those people that needed a rebuke and call them on their sin of gossip and slander.

God had vindicated us at our own wedding! It was so cool! We didn't need to do it or defend ourselves- God took care of it for us!

Mikey's Grandpa had told us before the wedding started that he wasn't sure about being the Pastor for our wedding and marrying us. He had heard so many negative things from Mikey's parents and from other family members that he wasn't sure if it was the right thing to do or even if it was God's will to marry us. He said that as he was getting ready before the wedding and getting his notes together for the ceremony that God's presence came on him and God spoke to him and showed him that it was His will. God gave him peace to do our ceremony and he was confident and sure of marrying us now that God had confirmed it to him! Side note: Whenever we, as humans, pray, ask God for help, and then truly trust Him, we can know He is faithful to answer us and bring vindication to His people. We don't need to worry about it or try to do it ourselves. He will do it! He is faithful!

We had a great wedding and an fun reception! We did our own hand-written vows, we gave each other our rings, we even shared our testimony about why we chose 2:22 as our time to get married, and we did communion together! Communion is one thing we really wanted to do. Communion is remembering Jesus and what He did for us. Without Him, there would be no us and no purity in our marriage, and no testimony. We wanted our wedding to honor Him! Without honoring Him and without His presence being there with us, what kind of wedding would that have been? Not a good one. The Lord's presence was there! Our friend, Josh, that did the d.j.ing picked an awesome song by Evan Earwicker for communion. It was such a perfect choice and brought us to tears of thankfulness. It reminded us of who God is and His love for us.

Newlyweds!

For the reception we didn't want to just do the traditional guarder belt thing. Mikey shook it up by washing my feet! He shared the Scripture about husbands washing their wives in the water of the Word. He said that the act of washing my feet on our wedding day was a symbol of what he would do every day of our marriage. It was so neat! Then he took off my guarder belt!

My new husband, Mikey!   Me, so happy on my wedding day!

Even in the midst of this wonderful day and time, the enemy tries to ruin it. We could not find the paper that had to be signed by the Pastor and two witnesses to say that we were now legally married. I just thought, okay, no big deal. We would find it after the reception or my parents would find it at home after the wedding and get it signed. I wasn't worried about it. However, during our reception Mikey's Grandma called us over and told us we had to have the paper right then. She said we weren't legally married until it was signed. She said we had to have it to be married and go on our honeymoon. She had me all freaked out. She had me thinking that if we left and went on our honeymoon without it being signed that we would be sinning since we, "Weren't really married." I know better now, but then I was so nervous. I didn't want to do anything wrong in God's sight, so I asked my Dad to go home right then and look at our house. My Mom went and looked up in the room where we got ready. I know now it would have been okay to go and just get it signed by his Grandpa and witnesses when we got back. In God's eyes we were married! The enemy will use people to try to ruin things just because he can if we let him. I wish now that I didn't let what his Grandma said make me nervous and worried about it. My Dad missed our Father-daughter dance because of it. That is one thing I wish I could do-over and not allow the enemy to affect my special day. My Dad and I have since made up the Father-daughter dance! It is okay. The enemy didn't win. We still had a wonderful day to the start of our new life together!

We left from the church and went on our honeymoon in Mandalay Bay, which is in Southern California. My Grandma blessed us by paying for our whole honeymoon! We had a great time just being together and finally being alone. We talked about our future together, prayed together, gave each other gifts, went out to eat, watched funny movies in our room and just laughed together! We felt free and so happy.

Once we got back from our honeymoon, we started work again. We both worked at a Christian camp called, "The Oaks." We worked together cleaning cabins, meeting rooms, and getting rooms ready for guests. We did this for several months and then I was getting very sick from all the chemicals and things we used to clean with. My husband wanted me to quit so I would not keep getting sick. So, I put in my two weeks notice and quit. Mikey continued to work hard to provide for us. I was a house wife, always keeping the house clean and making dinner for him. During the day when he was at work I had a lot of time to pray and read my Bible. The Lord used this time to prepare my heart to move.

CHAPTER THIRTEEN

"THE BIG MOVE!"

I would say about the time April rolled around, Mikey and I started feeling like we didn't want to be in California anymore. We had been born there and lived there our whole lives and we never thought of leaving. However, we started feeling a prompting from God like He wanted us to move out of state. We weren't sure where or why, but we knew in our spirits that He was doing something in us and causing us to want to move. So, of course, like always, we started praying for direction as to when and where.

We thought maybe He was moving us somewhere remotely close, like Washington or Nevada. The more we kept praying and seeking Him, we kept feeling like He was showing us Tennessee. At this time we really didn't know anything about Tennessee. We thought it was like all farm lands with no malls! Haha! We knew about Nashville on the West end of Tennessee, but not much about the East. We had heard of Nashville being "Music Central"- just like Hollywood is the "Movie Central". So, we thought maybe God was sending us there to do music. Mikey is a musician and I liked to sing so we thought maybe God was sending us to Nashville to do a music ministry or something like that. We weren't sure so we kept praying for more clarity as to where in Tennessee.

During this time, since I had quit working, Mikey got a second job at Smart and Final. He had this second job part time because he didn't want me to have to work. At this time of praying and seeking God and asking Him if Tennessee was for sure where He wanted us to go, Mikey started seeing all kinds of "Tennessee" signs at Smart and Final. I'll give you the first "sign" as an example to show you what I mean. His boss put Mikey in a section of the store where he never worked. He had to stock the shelves with alcohol. He noticed one of the boxes was in the wrong place, so he picked it up to move it and behind the box was a box of "Tennessee" Whiskey. He had never seen that brand before. If his boss hadn't needed him in that section that day, he would have never seen it. This sort of thing happened many times; all different "signs" God was using to confirm to us what we were already sensing in our spirits.

After so many times, we were finally like, "Okay, God, we get it!" You can say it is coincidence, but we don't believe in coincidences. We know that "coincidences" are acts of God choosing to remain anonymous; or sometimes not so anonymous. Not only did we keep seeing all kinds of "signs" pointing to Tennessee, but we could feel it and we knew this is where He wanted us. We knew it in our spirit. We still weren't sure why, but we knew we had to be obedient and we wanted to be obedient. His will is always the best, even if we don't understand everything. Now, after knowing He wanted us to move to Tennessee, we still prayed for direction and I had a dream. In my dream, I knew it was Jesus reaching His hand out to me. He said, "Just go and trust Me." Our flesh wants to know all the details first, but when we know Jesus the details don't matter. Well, I mean the details do matter, especially to God, but He will work them out as we go along. Being with Him and trusting Him is what really matters.

So, we started to pray about when to move and where in Tennessee. By this time I think it was about July. We felt we should move quickly, like there was an urgency in our spirits to move soon. Since we knew it would be soon, we figured we should probably tell our parents and families. One morning I went over to my parent's house. I was going to tell my Dad first that we were going to move out of state. While I was sitting there about to tell him, he got a phone call. I was nervous and holding back tears, knowing that this would be hard leaving my family. My Dad had his call on speaker. I don't remember the whole call, but I remember the guy he was talking to say, "Man, I have been all over the country and if there was anywhere I'd want to live, it would be East Tennessee." One more confirmation to me!

My Dad got off the phone and I told him what the Lord had shown us and told him we would be moving soon. He just smiled and said that the Lord had been showing them the same thing! What?! I expected him to cry and be upset that we were moving. Here he was smiling and saying that God told him they were to move as well!? I think it was even that same morning, during my Dad's prayer time in his closet, God had told my Dad they were supposed to move to Tennessee specifically! So, I was like, "Okay, cool!" I didn't have to worry about leaving them now because they were coming, too!

I went home and told Mikey that day when he got home from work and he couldn't believe it. He was excited because he was close to my family and wasn't looking forward to leaving them, either. So, now that we realized we were all moving, we started praying and looking for the specific city and house God wanted us to move to. When we would look on the computer for house searches, this "J.C." kept coming up. We thought it was funny, of course, because J.C. stands for Jesus Christ. We felt in our spirit like this was the city He was leading us to. He wanted us where "He was" so to speak, with the "J.C." We looked up J.C. and found out it stood for Johnson City. So, this is where we looked for houses. It was in East Tennessee like the guy my Dad had talked to mentioned on the phone.

Not so long after this (I believe it was that same week, on Sunday) my youngest sister, only three at the time, saw a vision of a "yellow house" in her Sunday school class. The teacher had them close their eyes and wait on the Lord to see what He would show them. She told her teacher she saw a "yellow house." This was still in July. Now, my Dad had found a huge house that him and my Mom really liked. It was big enough to allow room for Mikey and I to live with them, too, if we wanted. They said we could live with them. We thought that would be a good idea since we didn't really know the area yet and we didn't know where we wanted to get a permanent house. We did decide to do that so we could stay with them until we found jobs and a place of our own in Tennessee. We would have the downstairs, finished basement. We would have our own bedroom, bathroom, living room, music room, and half kitchen.

My Dad wanted to fly out and see this house in person before they purchased it. He flew out there with my sister, Misty, to see it and also look at some other houses while they were there. From the pictures online we could only see the front of the house and it was brick. When my Dad got there and saw the house, he called to tell us that the back of the house was yellow! Not just the back of the house, but the upstairs, inside was also a light yellow color! This confirmed that it was the house my youngest sister saw in her vision! We showed her the pictures and asked her if this was the house she saw and she said, "Yes." So, we prayed that if this was indeed God's will, that my parents would get the house that they would get it and quickly! They got it!

During this month of July, Mikey and I started packing by faith and we told our landlord we would be moving out soon. By the end of August, we were all packed and on our way driving to Tennessee! Mikey and I sold both of our cars so we would have money to move. We also did not think they would make it across country, as they were older, used cars. We knew that God would provide a vehicle for us when we got to Tennessee. Mikey and I drove my parent's van and they drove their SUV Kia and we followed each other on a five day journey across the country to our new home in Tennessee. It was such a fun and exciting time!

I want to throw something in here real quick. My youngest sister, Audrianna, who had the vision of the house, was a foster child. She was not adopted yet when we were getting ready to move. My parents received her in their home when she was just three months old. There was a fight for her life. The enemy tried to take her life several times. We all had been through a huge, ongoing battle for her life from day one until this point. We prayed that she would be adopted before we moved because if she wasn't it would be a huge, long ordeal to transfer everything to Tennessee and start from square one. There is so much to be said about this and I don't want to take too much time with it, but for more information about her story, read my Dad's book about it called, "No Idols." He has the whole story and testimony about her and her case. It is awesome! So, we prayed and long story short, Audrianna was adopted the DAY BEFORE WE LEFT! God is never late, although sometimes He has us wait till the very last second to test our faith and strengthen us! So, no kidding, we had court the day before we moved and she was able to be adopted and the case was closed before we left! God is such a big God!

Before I move on, you are probably wondering what Mikey's parents thought about this. Well, after we got married they didn't ever talk to us or come see us. When we knew we were moving we went over to their house to tell them in person. Mike was at work, so only Tammy was there for us to tell. We explained to her everything that happened and what God showed us and her response was, "Oh, so you're just following Lacy's parents there?" She walked out of the room mad and said some other negative comments to us. She didn't believe a word we said about how God showed us. She thought we were just moving because my parents were moving. That wasn't it at all. We were moving because God told us, too, and they just happened to be coming, too! I don't think we ever heard anything from Mike, except more negative words about how we won't know anybody and we won't make it and we'll never have enough money. We didn't see them until we went over there to say bye to them. After that, we moved!"

CHAPTER FOURTEEN

"TENNESSEE! A VEHICLE, JOBS, AND MORE!"

We arrived in Tennessee before our "stuff" did. We slept on blow up mattresses for a week and a half before our things arrived. My Dad worked from home at this time so he didn't have to look for work. Mikey and I needed jobs, however, so we began to pray and look for jobs. Before I get into our jobs, let me tell you how we got our car. We were out with my Mom one day after arriving in Tennessee. We went out to get cleaning supplies for the house so we could all start cleaning it. We drove by a Volkswagen dealership. I saw the prettiest turquoise blue "Hug Bug" I had ever seen. It was a brand new 2004 Volkswagen Beetle. For any of you who know me, you'll know that Volkswagen Beetles are my favorite cars! I had collected probably about 30 of them in my teenage years, all different sizes and colors. We needed a car. I saw this car turning around on one of those ramps on the front lot. I said to my Mom and Mikey, "That's my car right there!" My Mom and Mikey laughed, knowing I liked that car, but not thinking I was serious. I said, "One day that will be mine and I'll be driving it."

Now, I don't remember exactly how it all came about, but one day, shortly after this, we went to the dealership to inquire about the car. I had my parents come with us since we had no idea how to buy a car and we were still just newlyweds, not knowing how to do much on our own yet. My Dad also used to be a cars salesman so he could tell if the sales people were really giving us a good deal or trying to rip us off. I knew he would help us to bargain for a great price. After a while of talking to the dealers and taking it for a test drive, my Dad got them down to 1% interest and he got the price lowered with $500.00 cash back and satellite radio! Serious? Yes! What a deal! God not only provided us with a brand new car that was affordable, but also got it down to 1% interest. And not only that, but He provided us with instant $500.00 bonus cash that we needed until we found jobs and got our income rolling! The satellite radio was an added bonus!

The dealer that sold us our car was also a Christian. He was super honest and helpful. He made virtually no money from selling us this car because he got the price as low as it could possibly go, but he liked us and said he wanted to help us. Not only did he sell us our car, but we made a connection with him. He sends us Christmas cards and we are still friends to this day! This is just the beginning of how God used things, like this, in our life to connect us with people in Tennessee.

Okay, so back to getting a job. Mikey and I both applied at a restaurant really close to our house called "Cracker Barrel." We had never heard of it before, but it was close. We wanted to get something close to our house since we did not know our way around town yet and also to save on gas. We both applied, we both got interviewed together, and we both got hired together! The manager told us they don't allow married couples or people related to one another to work together because it could interfere with the job, but he said he liked us and wanted to give us a shot and hired us both! (More of God's favor!) We were thrilled. Mikey and I love to be together and I always wanted to have a job where I could be with him all the time (and not get sick like at our previous job). God answered our prayer and we got to train together and start together. They also told us that we probably wouldn't have the same shifts and that they would have to split us up, but we prayed that we would somehow be able to work together. I'd say about 95% of the time, we ended up having the same shift! We just about always worked together! God is awesome! It was so cool working together because it made work so much more fun and if one of us was tired or having a hard night, we could encourage each other right then!

We worked at Cracker Barrel for almost a year. During this time of working here we made many connections with different people; both from employees and customers, some of which we still talk to today. We were able to share our testimony over and over again about how the Lord lead us to Tennessee. Everyone knew we weren't from Tennessee. We were fresh out of California! The underneath of my hair was red and the top half of my hair was blonde! Mikey had his crazy spiked hair, which was definitely not the style out there! From the way we looked and the way we talked, everyone knew we weren't born there. The people told us we had "accents," when we thought they did!

God used our looks and speech to open the door for us to share about Him! Our guests that we served would say, "You're not from here are you?" Or "Where are you from?" We would say, "No, we are from California." Their eyes would always get big and then they would ask, "What made you move all the way here from California?" This would be our open door to share about how the Lord spoke to us to come here. From that point, there would be more questions to follow and we would be able to share about Jesus and give testimony about the Lord. We loved it! It was like we had our own little ministry at Cracker Barrel.

We became familiar with the "regulars" and they became familiar with us. We had people that would specifically ask for us when they came to eat. They would wait for a table to clear just so they could have me or Mikey for their server. They would tip us well! We made friends and connections. We had customers tell us that there was something "different" about us. They said they could feel God's love and/or "goosebumps" when we shared our testimony with them. (That was the Holy Spirit bearing witness in their spirit!) One lady even told Mikey that she saw a literal glow of a light in a circle all around him! People would give us things, i.e. their own personal valuable coins. God really blessed us there!

We were faithful to obey Him and move, even though we had no car, no money, no house, and we had no idea what to expect. (That's the fun of following the Lord!) We just went by faith, trusting Him that He would lead us and provide. He was faithful to meet us and to do just that! He provided a car for us right away, a job for us right away, a big place to live with my parents (until we found a place of our own), money, and the best part- He used us to share about Him! Mikey and I have always prayed for the Lord to use us as vessels for Him. There is no greater joy than serving Him and seeing people's lives changed because we shared Jesus with them. We got to encourage people just about daily! We were so happy working there and had so much joy! To be used by the Lord and watch Him open doors for us and lead us and provide for us was so exciting! I don't know how people find joy and purpose in life without Jesus, God, the Holy Spirit!

Chapter Fifteen

"Church"

After arriving in Tennessee, not only did we need to find a vehicle and jobs, but we also wanted to find a church. Driving through town one day, we saw a sign that read, "Hosanna Fellowship." We thought that it looked interesting. It wasn't your typical church building that you would see out here in Tennessee. Side note: The people here would tell us, "There's more churches than houses here in Johnson City." They weren't kidding. There are churches everywhere there. They are like McDonald's, one on every corner, if not more! LOL! Most all the churches there are your typical rectangle shape with a steeple on top. This church, Hosanna, had a weird kind on pentagon shape to it with no steeple. We thought, "That looks interesting and different, let's try it!" Of course we prayed for God to lead us to the right church during the time we moved until we found the right one. We had tried a couple churches already. When we went to Hosanna for the first time, we knew that it was where God wanted us. We could sense in our spirit that we were in the right place at the right time. (The "right place at the right time" just means being in God's will.) I think my family also came that Sunday, also, and decided they wanted to make this place their church family, too!

This church was similar to the church that we were going to in California. It was a non-denominational Christian church that believed in prophecy and things that are Biblical from the New Testament and held the same beliefs we did, too. The Pastor was also a Science teacher, so he had really good Science teachings that he would use to illustrate with. Not only did we get deeper teaching and knowledge of the Scriptures, but we also received basic 101 teaching in Science! At this church we also went to several studies and classes. We got involved in a "Watch and Pray" class, a "Dream Interpretation" class. We helped with the youth group, we both got on the worship team, and I was in a dance class. We had a very fun time of being a part of this church during this season. We also connected with several people and families that we became close friends with.

Our "Watch and Pray" class taught us how to be watchmen on the wall for our city. We went through Bible Scriptures to see what it meant to "watch and pray". It was very good and we grew a lot from the class. Our "Dream Interpretation" class was about how God speaks to us through our dreams. We learned how to pay attention to our dreams and how to ponder them and ask God what He was showing us through our dreams. We studied Daniel and some other Scriptures where God spoke to people through dreams. It was a very cool class and we learned some interesting things we didn't know before. Mikey played guitar for the worship team and occasionally drums. I sang. We helped with youth group on Wednesdays and with youth events. I was on a dance team for a while and then I actually taught a dance class for a season! It was super fun! We did a prophetic worship dance/dramatic presentation to the song "Some Trust in Chariots" by Todd Ganovski. It was so fun to put together and so powerful when we presented it!

I also want to add that God definitely knew what He was doing by leading us out to Tennessee and to this specific church. I think a major reason He had us there was to bring emotional healing to Mikey. Our Pastor had a very compassionate, Pastoral heart, as "Pastors" should have, and he poured in to Mikey's life and spirit. He stood in the place as Mikey's Dad one time (as the Lord lead him to), along with the associate Pastor and good friend of ours, to ask Mikey to forgive him. I remember them saying that they were standing in Mike's place to ask Mikey for forgiveness for all the hurt and rejection he caused Mikey. I remember Mikey balling and the two Pastors just held Mikey for the longest time. Besides that time, there were many other times they (or one of them) took Mikey to lunch, encouraged him in the Lord and also as a Father to a child, prayed for him, mentored him, etc. They were just there for him. They were like Father figures to Mikey and he absolutely needed that. God showed Mikey so much of His (the Father's love) through them and he gained a whole new healthy perspective of who God really is and how he really loved Mikey for who he was/is. It was a very beneficial time for us both, but especially Mikey. He loved those Pastors, became close to them, and still talks to them today!

During this time of working, going to and being a part of Hosanna Church, and getting used to Tennessee, we also got involved with Billy Wayne Ministries. In California, growing up every year, my family and I had a tradition with my Grandma and Grandpa to go see the "A Christmas Carol" play at the Glendale Theatre in Glendale, California every December. I had really missed going and I wanted to see if they did that play out in Tennessee. I also wanted to see it with Mikey. He never got to see it with us. The last time we went his parents didn't let him go with us because they thought he already spent enough time with me and my family for that week. I was so upset he couldn't see it with us. It was my favorite thing to do every year and I wanted to share that experience with him. I cried so hard and was so upset that he didn't get to see it with me, so I really wanted to still share this experience with him somehow.

I started looking online to see if there were any theaters out where we lived. I found a couple theaters by us and I looked in December to see if they did this same play. There was a theater in Fall Branch (about a half hour from us) called "Lamplight Theatre" that was doing an "Adaptation of A Christmas Carol"! I was so excited to find it. Mikey and I went that December. Friends of ours were there and they knew the owner of the theatre (who was also the main star of the play), Billy Wayne Arrington. Mikey wanted to meet him and our friends saw us there and said they knew him personally! They said, "Come on. We'll take you over to meet him." We met him and he immediately liked us. He said he saw something special in us. He asked Mikey if he played any instruments. He thought he did because he said Mikey looked like a musician. Of course Mikey told him yes and Billy asked him to come and play for him to sort of try out for his band.

We came back that next month and Mikey played for him. We also got to meet the other guys that were a part of his band. Of course Mikey played good and Billy liked him! He asked if he would be interested in traveling with him to play on his team and do ministry. I would be able to go, too, and help at the sales table or wherever I was needed. We went home and talked about it, prayed about it, and decided we wanted to do it. We felt that God connected us with him for a reason. We didn't quit our jobs. We kept working our normal jobs, but we would just request off for the weekends or week days when we would be out of town touring with him. God gave us favor and it was never a problem to get the time we needed off!

Just the two of us, having fun doing ministry!

It was very fun. We got to go to Pennsylvania, Maryland, Virginia, Florida, and some other nearby places. Mikey loved worshipping and playing with the guys. I ran the table where everyone could buy his shirts, rings, c.d.s, etc. I also got to talk to the kids and pray with some. We did this for about a year and we were asked if we wanted to do it permanently, full time and be paid for it. Although it was great traveling and being with other believers Mikey and I didn't like not being able to be together. What I mean by that is we were separated a lot by the ministry. He would have to set up the stage while I was setting up the table. He would have band practice while I sat and waited or went somewhere to pray. And the worst part was at night. We couldn't be in the same room. He had to be in the room with the guys and I had to be in a room with the other lady that came with us who was in charge of the finances. I guess this was due to being frugal with the money. They probably couldn't afford another room for just me and Mikey every time and plus it wasn't very fair to this lady for her to be by herself all the time. I could understand, but I didn't like it. Mikey and I had been torn apart and separated so much in the past from his parents, that I didn't like the feeling of being reminded of what that was like, neither did Mikey. So, we decided not to do it full time.

There was another factor, too. We really wanted kids. We really wanted to get pregnant and start a family. Since we shared that with Billy and the ministry, they kind of said they didn't want us to make a commitment to them and then we get pregnant and end up leaving after we've made a permanent commitment. They wanted a married couple that didn't have kids and weren't planning on having kids for a while. That wasn't us. We told them that we could continue with them until I would get pregnant and then take the time off we needed to have the baby. Then we could continue traveling with them after I healed and I could just bring the baby with us. They didn't think that I would be able to travel with a baby. They thought it would be too hard. So, that was that. We stepped down and they found someone else to take our spot. (And no hard feelings. We are still friends with Billy to this day.)

CHAPTER SIXTEEN

"THE FERTILITY PROBLEM"

Since the day Mikey and I got married, we wanted kids. We decided from day one of our marriage to ask the Lord for His timing and direction for us as to when He wanted us to have children. I was never on birth control and we didn't use condoms or any other sort of anti-pregnancy device. We wanted to fully trust the Lord in regards to this issue of children. We would always pray for God's perfect timing and will for when He wanted our kids to be born. At the beginning of our marriage we never "tried" to get pregnant, but we never "did not try", either. We thought it would be good for us to wait a little while before we had kids, but if we did get pregnant, then awesome! We didn't have a preference either way.

We trusted God that it would happen His way and in His timing. We would pray this: "Lord, let us get pregnant in Your timing, and if this is not your timing yet, then please close my womb or block the passage way so I will not get pregnant." We would always pray that way and pray for His will above what we wanted. And when there were times when we felt "not ready" for a kid, or felt it wasn't time yet, then we would just be careful and avoid sex around ovulation day. You can't get pregnant without ovulating (unless God does a miracle), so to not have a baby we just wouldn't have sex the day of, the day before, or the day after I ovulated. We chose to do this method because it was safe and it was what we felt was godly wisdom to avoid conception, instead of taking harmful birth control pills and other things that are bad for a women's body.

I had always been convicted about taking birth control pills. I had decided that when I got married I would never take birth control pills. Taking those pills is just an early abortion. As soon as you conceive, the pill kills the conception (the baby) and it just comes out of your body. My Mom used to work in a pregnancy crisis center. She learned about all that stuff and what the birth control pill really does. It doesn't stop you from getting pregnant, but once you get pregnant it kills the baby so you would never even know you were pregnant. So, knowing that, I could never justify taking the pills. I knew that would not honor God to kill a life He would give to me. So, I was always convicted to never take birth control, but to trust God fully in this matter. Mikey was on the same page with me and agreed with me and committed to trusting God with me, instead of relying on man-made chemicals to control the timing and destiny of our children. This is no condemnation to those taking birth control. It is a personal choice I (and my husband) made. You may have not known what birth control really is until now. Doctors and people sometimes lie to you to get you to take them.

So, anyhow, this is what we chose to do from the start of our marriage. People would tell us, "You need to go to college first, before you have kids." "You need to make more money and save up first, before you have kids." "You need to wait at least five years first, before you have kids." We heard all kinds of "advice"; worldly advice from Christians and unbelievers. We chose to listen to God's wisdom and His advice, rather than the wisdom of this world. We wanted to do His will more than what these people wanted for us, or thought was best for us. His will is best, whether that meant He gave us kids immediately or in 20 years! So, in short- one year went by, two years went by... and by this time we were starting to really want kids. We thought surely we should have been pregnant by now!? There were plenty of times we weren't "careful" that we should have became pregnant from.

So, after two years into our marriage, we started "trying" now. We had kind of, sort of tried in the past, but not consistently. So, we started charting ovulation, reading books on how to increase the chances of conception, praying, and tried to conceive. Another whole year went by and nothing. Three years into marriage and still no children. We were okay with that, but started getting concerned that maybe something was wrong with one of us. After all, three years of no birth control, no condoms, etc. you are bound to get pregnant, right?! And with a year of actually "trying" and still nothing... What was wrong with us? We still kept it in front of us and prayed to the Lord for direction, healing, etc. We also did the practical thing as well; we each saw a Doctor.

I went and had a test done to see if there was anything wrong with me, or anything holding me back from conceiving. I would always get really bad, severe cramps on my period, so the Doctors and some friends thought maybe I had cysts on my ovaries. I had a pap test and an ultra sound of my ovaries and everything was normal. All the tests came back great and there was nothing wrong with me. I was clear for take-off! So, I went with Mikey and they tested him. They called back with the report. They had tested his sperm for all different kinds of things; numbers, mobility, strength, etc. They said he was okay, but that his numbers were a little lower than "normal." Their mobility was a little on the slower moving side and his count was a little lower than normal. They said that could be hindering the conception somewhat, but he wasn't infertile or anything "bad" or "wrong" where we couldn't have kids.

We didn't necessarily want to see Doctors, but we so desperately wanted to get pregnant that we were willing to go to a Doctor. And we also wanted to go for the sake of having a written document of what was or wasn't wrong with us. If something was wrong with either of us and there was a negative report saying that we couldn't have kids, we wanted to hold on to it so that when we did get pregnant we could show people and give glory to God for His miracle. We knew and believed that even if something was wrong with us that God could heal us and give us children anyway. The Doctor's report would prove that we couldn't, but God could!

With nothing majorly wrong with either of us, we kept praying for God's timing and will. We knew He wanted us to have children. We had been given prophecies from several different people that didn't know us saying, "I see the Lord wants to bless you with children. I see kids playing the drums and running around playing." We had received several words like that. And God's word also says to, "To be fruitful and multiply..." so we knew it was His will for us to produce and have offspring, but when? We also did practical things like go to the Health Food Store and ask for teas and herbs that would help increase sperm mobility and boost conception chances, etc. Sometimes I would wonder if I was getting impatient and trying to take matters into my own hands by taking herbs and vitamins and things. I think that can happen, but I know that I did trust God to allow it to happen in His timing. I just wanted to prepare my body, physically, too, in the mean time (and so did Mikey). I wanted to be ready to conceive and do anything possible on my part to show God I am prepared and ready to receive His blessings.

Chapter Seventeen

"FOSTER CARE"

Now we were getting close to three and a half years of not getting pregnant and still hoping and believing for kids of our own one day. At this same time we had someone come to our church and share with us about the need for foster care. We prayed about it, talked about it, and decided we wanted to be foster parents in the hopes of adopting. This was not because we lacked faith in God giving us our own children. It was from a desire to have kids to take care of, even if they weren't from us. We wanted to adopt, even if we did have our own. So, after praying, and feeling peace about it from the Lord, we wanted to be foster/ adoptive parents in the mean time while waiting on the Lord for our own.

We started our foster care training that year in the Fall of 2007. We were at three years and 10 months with no children at this point. We did all of our foster care training every Saturday from like 8:00 a.m.-1:00 or 8:00 a.m.-3:00 for about two months. Once we completed our training, we prayed and waited for a call to get a child placement, but we never got a call. God had it on hold. We were now certified foster parents, but we were not getting any calls for child placements.

Also, during this time, one of our friends from California asked if he could come stay with us for a while. He had been struggling in his walk with Christ and wanted to "get away" from everything. He wanted to get away from the negative influence and come stay with us for a few months in hopes we would encourage him and help him get back on his feet and also encourage him in his relationship with God. So, we said okay and he came and stayed with us from November 2007 until February 2008. We did minister to him and joked that he was our "foster child" for the time being!

During this same time, in February 2008, my Mom and Dad were doing foster care as well. They would take kids into their home to stay and they would take care of them until their parents got back on their feet. Sometimes parents struggled and couldn't ever get their lives together, so the kids would go up for adoption. My parents would then pray if they should adopt those kids or not. At this time, they had just taken in two little girls; sisters. I'm not sure if I'm allowed to use their real names, so I will use fake names. Ann was 2 1/2 and Mary was eight months old. They were both overweight and behind developmentally. My parents cared for them from February to May. My Mom had also started getting rheumatoid arthritis around this time. Her hands were getting worse and it was physically hard for her to take care of the girls. She could hardly change the baby's diaper and get her dressed. With that being so hard, along with all the emotional and behavioral challenges, they decided they couldn't keep the girls.

Knowing they were going to give the girls back into another foster home and seeing as how we wanted kids, Mikey and I thought, "Why don't we take the girls?" After all, they already knew us now and it would be a lot better for them to come stay with someone they already knew, rather than go into another strange, new home. Mikey and I prayed about it and then started our foster care training at the agency where these girls were placed in. I believe it was God's will that we didn't get a call for any children from Fall of 2007 until Spring of 2008 because then we would have had other kids already and would not have been able to take in Ann and Mary.

Okay, so it was now Spring of 2008. The girls were in a different agency than we were in. In order to consider getting the girls placed with us, Mikey and I had to switch all our paper work over to this other agency and redo CPR training and First Aid training, etc. We completed everything and proceeded to ask if the girls could transfer to our house. My Mom also told them how she could no longer care for the girls. They weren't sure we could get the girls, but we knew the power of prayer and what our God can do. We prayed. And after several meetings with the agency and with DCS and the social workers, they finally got the upper hand approval to move the girls to our house! We were so excited! On May 27th, 2008 Ann and Mary were placed in our home! Ann had just turned three and Mary was now 11 months old.

At this point, Mikey and I were both working full time. I was the Manager at Great American Cookies in Bristol, Virginia and Mikey worked as an Electrical Apprentice for Marty's Electric here in Johnson City, Tennessee. My schedule was pretty flexible. Since I was the manager I could make my own schedule. We did not want to put the girls in day care after all they had already been through, so we worked it out to work opposite shifts. Usually, Mikey worked in the mornings while I cared for the girls at home and when he got home, we switched. I went to work in the afternoon/night and he stayed home and cared for the girls. Most days I had my shifts from 2:00 p.m. until 10:00 p.m. and Mikey typically worked 8:00 a.m.-4:00, but now he would have to leave early to get home in time for me to get to work by 2:00. I was off on Thursdays, so he would work late on Thursdays to make up some hours and also get some hours in on Saturdays.

I know the last thing I left off with, as far as work goes, is that we were working at Cracker Barrel. After almost a year, we quit. They had a smoking section at that time (back in the day... lol) and we had to rotate shifts to work in it. The smoke really was starting to bother me and also make me and Mikey sick. We asked if we could not have to work in the smoking section, but they said no. We had prayed about whether or not to continue working there. Mikey had a dream. The very next day everything in the dream happened! I mean like exactly! It was like deja vu for Mikey. He was re-living what already happened in the dream. Anyway, I won't go into the dream, but let's say it was God showing us it was in fact time to quit working there. I went on to get an Assistant Manager's position at Great American Cookies for 2 1/2 years in Johnson City and then got promoted to store Manager in Bristol. Mikey had several different jobs in a row that had to do with construction work and was now doing electrical work.

CHAPTER EIGHTEEN

"MOVING TO KNOXVILLE?!"

We did this same routine from May 27th until the very end of August, so for a little over three months. During this same time, since the first of January this year, 2008, we had been going to a church in Knoxville, Tennessee, about two hours away from us. We felt God lead us there at the end of December 2007. We had been going to Hosanna Fellowship (the first church we became a part of since we moved to Tennessee) for three and a half years already and we loved it, but now God was leading us somewhere else. This church in Knoxville that God had now led us to was a non-denominational Christian church. We would go out to Knoxville for church, eat lunch out there, and then come home. After four hours of driving to church and back every week, for these eight months, we felt God leading us to move there. We started looking for houses or apartments to rent. Mikey started looking for a job. We put in our notices at our current work places. We told our agency about what we were planning and they said it would be next to impossible to get an okay for our foster girls to move two hours away, out of their county.

You know what we did? Prayed! If this was God's will for us to move and be able to keep the girls, He would make a way and it would get approved. This was a very emotional time for me. I knew what the agency and social workers kept telling us, that they would not allow the girls to move with us that far away, but I also knew God was wanting us to move to Knoxville. I was so upset because I didn't want to move if that meant we would lose the girls, but I also knew I had to obey God above my emotions and what I wanted. This was a real test for me to be obedient to God and what He wanted for us, whether the girls came with us or not. Although the girls had only been with us for three months, we had already bonded with them so well. We already felt like they were our own children and I couldn't imagine going back to life without them. I went through a lot of emotional ups and downs and cried a lot during the few weeks of decision making by the agency and DHS. It was definitely a time of learning how to truly trust God... again! And also how to put God first, above all else!

After a couple of meetings with us and the agency; the agency and DCS and DCS with us, trying to get the approvals, and Mikey and I trying to convince them that the girls would be better off with a house change, not a people change- they finally approved it! (What I mean by "a house change, not a people change" is although either way it would be another new change for the girls, they would be better off staying with the same people they know and just moving to a new house, rather than moving in with strangers again. Then they would not only be in a new house, but also have to get used to new people.) So, they finally approved the girls to move to Knoxville with us! It was close to the last minute, right before we had to move.

While driving around in Knoxville one day, we saw a sign for a duplex to rent. We called on it and looked at it. It was a huge one story house with wood flooring, new carpet, and two oversized bedrooms; each with their own bathroom! Mikey loved it right away. I had some concerns with it being a duplex. For example, there was one staircase we would share with the neighbors on the other side. That staircase went down to the garage and laundry room. We each had our own garage and laundry room, but I was nervous about sharing a staircase. What if the neighbor was a single guy or a rapist or something? I didn't want to walk out when he did and something happen to me or the girls. Call it fear or real concern, I wanted to make sure it was safe. The landlords assured me it was safe. They said their daughter was using the other side as storage and was normally not even home. So, I felt better knowing that.

We also had found an apartment by the mall. It was $787.00 a month for a two bedroom, but was only about 500 square feet. The duplex was 1,800 square feet for only $800.00! So, more than three times bigger for only $13.00 more seemed like an obvious no brainer. However, I was still really debating about which place would be better. I was praying about it. I liked the apartment, although it was small, because it was closer to town and it had a pool. I liked the duplex because there was much more space. After praying and talking it over, Mikey decided the duplex would be best. He felt God lead us there and that's where he decided we should be. I still wasn't 100 percent settled with it because it was further away from his work and town and because of the whole duplex idea, but I happily submitted and became more and more okay with it as we packed and started moving!

CHAPTER NINETEEN

"NEW CHURCH, NEW KIDS, NEW HOUSE, NEW JOB!"

At this time of finding a house, Mikey still had not found a job, although he had put in many applications. We still continued to pack and move by faith, knowing this is where God was leading us. We knew He would provide the right job for Mikey! One day, while I was still working at the cookie company, one of my faithful morning coffee customers came by for his morning coffee. I told him we were going to be moving soon and that I would no longer be here to serve him coffee. I told him I had put in my notice and that another manager would come take my spot. He asked me where and why I was moving. I told him Knoxville and explained how the Lord was leading us there. He asked what job my husband had got out there. I told him he hadn't found one yet, but we were believing God to provide one. He told me to have Mikey apply at Food City because his son was the district manager over that area and that he would put in a good word for Mikey and I. So, Mikey put an application in at the specific Food City he told us about.

Mikey did not have any management experience at this time, except for assisting me at the cookie place for a short time. He didn't want to be a cashier or bagger. He knew he was capable of more than that and we needed more pay than what those positions payed. So, with prayer and in faith, Mikey applied for a "Front-End Manager" position. After persistent calling and two interviews, he was hired for that management position! My coffee customer said he forgot to put in a good word for Mikey, and that was okay. God still gave Mikey the job. I think that my coffee customer telling us about Food City was just God's way of getting

Mikey to apply there because that is definitely where He wanted Mikey. We would have never thought of applying there ourselves.

Mikey learned so much while working at Food City. The Lord taught him so many things there; both mentally in dealing with employees and customers and by learning how to manage, and also taught him spiritually how to identify things going on and how to deal with people spiritually. He got many raises while he was there and also received awards for customer care. The Lord blessed him with favor, even with an unbelieving boss. Also, sweet little ladies would always give him monetary tips from $1.00- $20.00 at a time! He was always blessed there. I forgot to mention this, but when we moved to Knoxville, I did not look for a job. We decided that I should stay home full time now to take care of our foster daughters. So, Mikey was at this job for four years. This whole time I was a stay at home Mom taking care of our foster girls.

Chapter Twenty

"A Baby!"

After moving to Knoxville in August, we attended a Christian conference that our church hosted there in Knoxville, in September. There was a speaker/Prophet there named Bob Jones. After worship on the first night of the conference, Bob came up on the stage and said, "There is someone here who has been trying to have children, but has not been able to. If that is you, stand up." There were probably about 300 to 400 people there. I think he said again, "There are three of you or several of you trying to conceive and are not being able to. If it is you, stand up." So, of course I stood up and already started to get emotional because I knew the Lord heard my prayers and was healing me. Bob continued, "There is a seal placed over your womb. I see it in he spiritual realm. There is a seal over your womb and it has prevented the sperm from getting through to fertilize the egg." Yes, he said it that graphically! He said, "Place your hands on your womb." I did. And he continued, "I break that seal now in the name of Jesus Christ. It is broken now. You should be able to feel warmth in your womb now." So, when I placed my hands on my womb and agreed in prayer with Bob, thanking God, I could feel a slight warmth in that area. I knew God was touching me. So, just to be clear- he never laid hands on me. He stayed up on the stage and I was in my seat- about two rows back from the front. God healed me, not Bob. Bob was used as a vessel to bring that word of knowledge and pray for me.

After that, Bob encouraged us not to doubt that the Lord has healed us and to believe by faith now that we would conceive. I was so excited and overwhelmed by God's love for me. I was so thankful for my healing and I really did believe, without doubting, that I would conceive now. I was overwhelmed that God saw my hurt and faith in the midst of all the hundreds of people that were there and that He pointed me out to heal me and make me a testimony of His love, healing, and what He can do! He is a big God that sees all of our problems and loves us enough to help us overcome them- if and when we let Him.

After this conference, I shared what happened with my family over the phone, since they were still living in Johnson City. They were like, "Cool, that's exciting!" My Mom still warned me to not "get my hopes up" because this didn't mean that I would conceive immediately. Even though I was healed it might still be "months or years from now". I know her intention was for me not to be disappointed if I did not get pregnant right away, but I knew that was not faith. I was believing I would get pregnant right away, or next to right away. I was healed now! What could prevent pregnancy now?!

The very next month, on October 28th- my husband's birthday, I conceived!

Me- ecstatic to be pregnant!

November 10th was my birthday and it also happened to be the first day of my missed period! I figured I was probably pregnant because I was never late for my periods, but I was nervous to do the pregnancy test. I waited a few more days. Sure enough, a few days/nights later I still hadn't started and I was so anxiously excited that I took the pregnancy test and it was positive! I was so excited! Mikey was right there with me and I smiled and he knew and said, "Really?! Are we?!" He hugged me and was so excited! We both started getting teary eyed and thanked God. We were ecstatic! It was so surreal and hard to believe because there had been so many times I thought I might have been pregnant and I took the test and it was always negative. There had been many disappointments and times of hurting. To see a positive sign, it was hard to believe and take in. And let me just add in here that we did not "try" this month. We simply just enjoyed each other on my husband's birthday and it just so happened to be ovulation day! I guess that was God's birthday gift to Mikey and also my birthday gift to find out on my birthday! Isn't God so cool! His timing is outstanding!

My friend told me how to calculate my due date. She said, "Go back three months from the first day of your last period and add seven days to it. That is your due date." So, I figured out my due date and I found out that it was July 22nd of 2009. At first I didn't think anything of that due date. Just another day, I thought, but then I remembered a prophecy I had received from a lady that didn't know me- from 2001! I got out the card that she had written my prophesy on. It said, "Does the date July 22nd mean anything to you? It will be a significant date for you to remember." I knew this was the significant date that she was talking about! It was now being fulfilled- eight years later! Isn't God amazing? He orchestrates everything perfectly to make sure we know it is Him mapping out our life perfectly!

Some people questioned my conception date. Let's just say I know when I have sex with my husband, and not only that, but I tracked my period, ovulation, etc. The lady at the health clinic, where I applied for my insurance, also gave me the conception date of Oct. 28th or 29th and a due date of July 22nd or 23rd according to the first day of my last period and according to the little chart she had. I was sure!

Now, I want to go back for a minute. About two years earlier, in Fall of 2006, Mikey and I were in our little cottage in Johnson City and we were praying about our kids. We were asking God who are kids would be when we had them. We asked Him to show us what to name them and prayed for them. One night while doing this, the Lord spoke to Mikey and said, "I want you to name your firstborn son Ezekiel Daniel." Just how it is laid out in the Bible; Ezekiel Daniel. We said okay. I liked the name Ezekiel, but I didn't really like the name Daniel because I thought it was too common. It wasn't something I would have picked, but nonetheless, we chose to do God's will, not our own. We said okay and knew that meant we would have a son someday.

So, now that we were finally pregnant, we thought for sure I was carrying a boy. I just knew it was a boy since the Lord had given us a boys name. Everyone else kept telling me I was having a boy, too. Mikey's parents kept saying it was a boy. This nurse at Mikey's work said she could tell by how I was carrying the baby that it was a boy. Finally, the time came for the mid-prenatal ultra sound. The sonographer says, "It's a GIRL!" I'm like, "What? Are you sure?" I started crying! Of course I was happy still, even though it was a girl, but I was in complete shock! Mikey and I thought for sure we were having a boy and had kind of planned for a boy. And, I already had two girls! Ann and Mary were my girls and I was kind of ready for a boy now!

After the shock of the baby being a girl set in and I finally calmed down, I was excited! Mikey and I had to gear up for a girl now. We had a couple of girl names that we had picked a while ago. You know, we thought for the future, later on when we would have a girl after our boy! LOL We prayed about it and asked God what to name her. We really liked the name Alexia! We liked the meaning of the name and we thought it was unique and pretty. In the Bible it says, "A good name is to be chosen rather than great riches," Proverbs 22:1a NKJV." The meaning of the name is much more important than what the name sounds like. "Alexia" means, "Defender of Mankind," and "Benefactor." The Scripture for that name is Isaiah 1:17 NKJV "Learn to do good; Seek justice, Rebuke the oppressor; Defend the fatherless, Plead for the widow." Great verse!

We felt that this is what God wanted us to no name our daughter. We felt she would be a benefactor to others and defend mankind, especially the helpless and the weak. After we decided this, we received many prophetic words from different people describing who our daughter would be and all the words matched what her name meant and confirmed to us what God showed us. For her middle name, we wanted to name her Jade. Jade means "Precious," and "Priceless Gem." We wanted her to know that she was always precious and priceless to us and to God. My youngest sister's middle name is also Jade and I thought it would also be neat to name her after my sister. Her name is Audrianna Jade and our daughter would be Alexia Jade, so they would both be "A.J.'s" for short!

July 22nd, 2009 came around; my due date, and nothing happened! I thought for sure she would be born on her due date since that date was prophesied eight years ago! Nope, she was born 11 days "late" on Sunday, August 2nd, 2009 at 10:52 a.m.! She was 21 inches long and weighed eight pounds even! I didn't understand why she wasn't born on that special day in July, and instead became an August baby. The Lord showed me why later on, but I won't get into that yet. And just to let you know, I did have a great pregnancy! A hard labor and delivery that lasted four days, but it was worth it! With the Lord's strength I had her naturally with no epidural! After three days of labor I was not progressing past three centimeters, so on the fourth morning, I finally went to the hospital and they gave me Pitocin to speed up the process and then broke my water. After that, I dilated to 10 centimeters and then pushed for three and a half hours! Then, she finally came out- healthy as can be! Praise God!

I also want to add something else here that is very important! I gained two new brothers and a sister shortly after Alexia was born! In December, 2009, my parents adopted three teenagers/kids that they had been fostering! Daniel, James, and Ashley. Daniel and James were half brothers; same Mom, different Dad. Ashley was from a different family altogether. They were 16- Ashley, 15- Daniel, and 11- James at the time of adoption! So, with the three of them added to our family, I now had six siblings; three sisters and three brothers!

Mikey, me, and our sweet baby, Alexia Jade! One month old.

Chapter Twenty-One

"LIFE GETS BUSY"

At this time, we still had our foster girls. They were there at the hospital with us while I gave birth to our daughter and they saw Alexia right after she was born! We still intended to adopt them! Just because we had our own daughter now didn't mean we were done doing foster care. They had been with us for over a year and two months now and we still wanted to and had every intention of adopting them.

They adapted to the change of a new baby at home fairly well. Ann (the older one) did especially well with Alexia and loved to hold her. Ann was now four years old and Mary had just turned two in June. Our three girls were all two years apart! As Alexia got older, Ann liked to take care of her and play with her. Mary had a little bit of a harder time (probably because she was younger) and would be rough with Alexia. Sometimes she would push Alexia. They were closer in age and she didn't quite understand the new baby thing.

For the next year and four months (16 months) I had three girls to take care of at home! We celebrated Ann's fifth birthday together, Mary's third birthday together, and Alexia's first birthday together! During this time, and as the foster girl's got older, they started exhibiting a lot of behavioral problems and learning problems. We knew from the start that they were delayed behaviorally and delayed in speech because of the parent's drug use and neglect. However, as time went on through my pregnancy and during the first year of our daughter being here with them, more and more things started surfacing and becoming apparent as to how far the girls really were behind and how many issues they had from being drug babies.

Because the girls were behind in speech, we had to take both Ann and Mary to speech therapy twice a week. They were also behind physically. Their muscles weren't very strong. They couldn't do certain physical activities that any "normal" kid could definitely do by their age. We had to start taking them to physical therapy once a week (sometimes twice a week) to work on that. Ann couldn't do certain motor skills so she had to go to occupational therapy once a week. We didn't mind taking them to these appointments and therapies because we wanted to help them get caught up to where they needed to be. However, it was a lot of work! Not only did we take them to therapy, but then there were activities and "homework" we had to do with them at home to help. That was fine, too, since it gave us some one and one time with them!

We would set up their appointments on Thursdays when we could. Thursdays were Mikey's day off. I wanted him to come with me to the appointments to help me. I could watch and take care of Alexia myself when both the girls were in an appointment session, but when Ann just had an appointment it was hard for me to watch both Alexia and Mary. Mary was not a calm child. She liked to bang her head in the stroller and scream and spit and run. If I was holding my baby, I couldn't chase after her or calm her down all the time. Mikey also wanted to come with me to help me. He liked spending time with all of his four girls and he knew I needed help and he liked being there for me. A lot of their appointments were twice a week so I would usually take them on Tuesdays by myself and on Thursdays with Mikey.

Now, not only were we running them to speech therapy, physical therapy, and occupational every week, but then we had their regular Doctor appointments for well check ups and their dentist appointments for teeth cleanings. Then, I also had to go to Alexia's Doctor appointments for well visits. And the girls qualified for W.I.C. from being foster children, so I had to take them to WIC appointments. And on top of all these appointments, Mary's head was larger than it was supposed to be! Her Doctor was concerned about that, and so were we, so her Doctor referred her to a specialist. The specialist also confirmed that her head was too big for her age. We thought it might be a tumor or something, but we were praying it wasn't. They had her head tested through a cat scan and they didn't see any tumors or anything to be concerned about. They still wanted to keep an eye on her head growth though, as she got older, so we had to keep going back to that specialist periodically for head measurements and check-ups.

On top of that they both had to see a neurologist specialist because of how far they were behind developmentally. This neurologist was the one that actually referred Ann to have occupational therapy. We would have to go see her periodically to have them re-checked to see if all their therapies were working and to see if their skills were improving. She also did brain exercises with them at their appointments and showed us brain activities that we could do with them at home. And these appointments I am mentioning were not quick. They were almost always about two hours long! They were not fun, especially trying to keep my own baby happy and busy for two hours while watching the girls and learning what I needed to do with them at home.

As if all of this wasn't enough, both of the girls exhibited signs of autism. I picked up on it and their Doctor picked up on it at their well check-up visits as well. They would stare at kids, instead of interacting and playing with them. Mary would bang her head on the wall often. They didn't communicate well. They would have little idiosyncrasies that they would do over and over again. Instead of playing with toys, Mary would destroy them. Instead of playing with toys, she would rather pick off pieces of our blinds and eat them. (Just to be clear, I did watch them! She would eat the blinds and things like that during her nap time when she was supposed to be sleeping. I would come check on her and find her doing things like that!) We picked up on those odd behaviors and Mikey and I thought they weren't "normal" behaviors. Mikey and I didn't have kids before them, of course, so we didn't really know what "normal" was for their age, but from what we knew from observing other kids, and from our own logic, it didn't seem normal.

I just want to throw in here that they did not fully show signs of autism until the state demanded that we "catch up" on all their vaccinations. They had not done all these weird behavioral things prior to getting their shots; Mary, especially. She had to get five or six shots at one time after she turned 18 months old. After that, she was a different kid. I am not telling you what to think or do regarding vaccinations, but just think about that for a while.

The girls were referred, by their Doctor, to a phycologist specialist for autism testing. I was with them when she did their testing. It was so short of a time that she was with each of them, I don't know how it was enough time to observe them and test them, but after about a half an hour she diagnosed them. She said they definitely did show some "odd behaviors." She said they weren't full blown autistic, but that they were borderline autistic, like aspergers. She said they were on the mild side of the scale and said they had "Pervasive Development Disorder." So, now we also had to go to her for therapy so she could work with the girls on that disorder!

We also had a referral from their Doctor for a place called, "Helen Ross". They had to go there to see a Psychiatrist specialist to get medicine. The girls wouldn't sleep, especially the older one. They would stay up late in the night, get up super early, and not take a nap the majority of the time. This was mostly a problem for the older one. But, as the younger one got older, and from the influence of her older sister keeping her up, it became a problem with her, too. We would have a nightly routine and try to get them to be by 8:00 or 8:30 every night. We thought that was a reasonable time for a one year old and three year old to go to bed at night. The problem is that the majority of the time they wouldn't go to sleep! They would be up until 9:00 p.m., 10:00 p.m., 11:00 p.m., midnight... Even on the nights they fell asleep at a somewhat of a decent time, they would be up again at 12:30 a.m. or 1:00 a.m. in the morning! They would never call for us or come get us. They would just get out of bed and play. I remember one night (actually more than one night) we woke up to hear them running in the kitchen! And another time- playing in the bathroom sink. And other times- just running around or in each other's rooms playing.

This was exhausting! Not only were we already tired from having three kids to take care of (including a new baby of our own), but we were exhausted from running to countless appointments all throughout the week, and now we were getting even more exhausted from them waking us up during the night! After more than a year of all these issues with the girls and a plethora of appointments, it was now starting to wear on us! This "season" we were in started becoming a real frustrating time for us. The girls were on Melatonin to help them sleep, which eventually stopped working. I think their bodies became desensitized to the medicine. Then they were on a more serious sleep drug to help them go to sleep and to stay asleep during the night. Sometimes it seemed to work, sometimes it didn't. We didn't know what else to do to help these girls. Of course we would pray over them every night! We would make sure they were full. We would read to them, make them warm tea, etc. Whatever we could think of to do to help them sleep, we would do, but nothing seemed to work.

We would give them naps during the day between 1:00 p.m. and 3:00 p.m. because they were so tired, grouchy, and fussy from not sleeping very much during the night. (Not that they would always take their nap, but we had them at least lay down and try!) We also gave our daughter a nap during this same time every day. It was supposed to be my quiet time where all three girls would sleep and I could pray, read my Bible, and just have some quiet. My daughter would always take her nap. Sometimes the girls would take their nap and sometimes not. A lot of times I would check on them and they would be awake. I don't know how they kept themselves awake when they were so tired, but they would. A lot of times, Ann would just be sitting up in her bed or playing with her toys, instead of laying down and being obedient. Mary would usually be destroying her toys or climbing on her window seal or jumping out of her crib (and later bed), or pooping in her pull-up and smearing it on her walls and floor. You know, whatever was more fun than taking a nap! Mary was more defiant and usually was doing something destructive, dangerous, or gross. Ann was more calm.

I was real worried about Mary. I didn't want her to get hurt. We took care of the crib problem by getting her a normal toddler bed that was low to the floor. The window seal thing we couldn't help. We moved everything away from her window, but she would still find some way to get up there and jump off. I watched the girls all day and Mikey and I played with them all the time, but I did need a break and some rest each day. Their nap time was my short amount of time when I would get a break. We tried not to schedule appointments around that time, either. Even though their nap time was from 1:00-3:00 it usually only lasted about an hour. I would have to intervene or let them out of their rooms before they got hurt of ruined more of our stuff or their toys. I didn't feel comfortable leaving them in their room for naps, but I had to. I needed some down time and they needed some quiet time to chill. Once in a while they would actually sleep so then I wouldn't have to keep checking on them every five minutes!

Chapter Twenty-Two

"BUSY, BUSY, BUSY!"

Since Ann and Mary were foster girls, they had social workers. They had one from the state (from DCS) and one from the agency we went through. They were required to come to our house and visit with the girls at least twice a month. Sometimes they would come together, but most of the time they came at separate times. I had to fit their home visits into our already busy schedule. And since we were foster parents, we had to attend regular trainings every month in Kingsport (which was two hours away)! We had to go on Thursdays and on some Saturdays. Oh, ya, and let's not forget about going to all the court cases. We had to go to court to testify and to see what was going on with the parents and to see if the judge would terminate the parents' right so we could adopt them. Oh, and the Helen Ross place, where they saw the psychiatrist for their medicine, they also assigned Ann a home social worker to come see her in the home twice a week to help her with her behavioral issues.

Okay, so by now you've got to be getting a picture of how busy our life was in order for us to take care of our foster daughters and make sure they were getting all the help they needed. In hinds sight, I think one of the reasons God had us move to Knoxville was for them. All the specialists the girls saw were located in Knoxville. If we were still in Johnson City, we would have had to drive all the way to Knoxville to every one of their appointments! We would never be home! They don't have the kind of specialists the girls needed in Johnson City. It was already hard enough trying to get to all their appointments every week when they were nearby. Well, except for their speech. Their speech was in Oak Ridge and it took us almost an hour to get there every week. The other appointments were fairly close- between 15 to 30 minutes away.

One more thing I didn't mention yet. Mary was not learning to go potty on the toilet, no matter what method I used. She was already three at the time when I figured, "She should be potty trained by now!" She would pee so much it seemed excessive to me. She would soak those potty training "big girl pants" like nothing. I remember we took her to the Doctor one day because she was sick and they had her do a pee test. The test came back not so good. There was protein in her urine and it wasn't supposed to be there. The Doctor was concerned that maybe something was wrong with her kidneys. They referred us to a kidney specialist. We went to the kidney specialist and there was indeed a problem with her kidneys. I don't remember the specific diagnosis, but it had to do with the protein in her urine. The specialist said that might be why she is not potty trained. She might not be able to hold her urine until she makes it to the toilet. She put Mary on medication for it. We had to check back with this specialist periodically to make sure her kidneys were okay and didn't get worse.

I know I just threw a lot out there as you were reading right now. So, let me re-cap and summarize everything I just wrote about so you have an understanding of what Mikey and I were going through at this point and what we started feeling. Between all three girls we had regular Doctor appointments (two different Doctors/two different places because Alexia went to a different place than the girls did), dentist appointments, WIC appointments, a psychologist, a psychiatrist, a neurologist, a kidney specialist, a genetics specialist (for Mary's head), two state social workers, one Helen Ross social worker, court dates, and foster care trainings. Besides that, we still did all the "normal life" things like go to church, grocery shopping, errands, etc.

A typical week might look like this: Monday- DCS social worker coming for a home visit from 9:00-9:30. Then off to the neurologist at 10:00. We'd get out of there by 12:00 and be starving for lunch. We'd get lunch, then go home for nap at 1:00. Mikey would get home at 2:30 and we'd leave by 3:00 to go grocery shopping. Come home and make dinner. Then the Helen Ross social worker would come for a home visit from 5:30-6:00. Then we would give the girls a bath and then play with them and work on their activities with them. Then we would worship and have prayer time and go to bed. Tuesday- Morning speech appointments and physical therapy appointments from 8:30-9:30. Then morning psychologists appointments for both girls from 10:00-11:00 and then head on over to occupational therapy from 11:30-12:00. Then lunch and nap. Then we would leave to go to the psychiatrist appointment at 3:00. Mikey would meet us there. That would last till 4:30. Home to make dinner. While we would be trying to make dinner, a Helen Ross social worker would come for another visit from 4:30-5:00. Then bath time, play time, and learning time, prayer, and bed. Wednesday- Agency social worker would come for a home visit from 9:00-9:30. Then we would leave to see the genetics Doctor at 10:00. We would get out of there by 11:45. Then lunch and home for nap.

After nap, we would go run errands and get the girl's prescriptions filled. Then, home for dinner and repeat our routine from Monday and Tuesday night.

Thursday- Alexia's well check up at her Doctor at 10:00. We would be done by 11:00. Then we would go straight to the dentist for the girl's cleaning appointments at 11:15 (drive fast... lol). Be done by 12:15. Lunch and home for nap. After nap, we would drive straight to Oak Ridge for their speech from 4:00-5:00. Then come home for dinner and our nightly routine. Friday- In the morning, take the girls to go get a toy and spend their allowance money. Then take them to Babies "R" Us to shop for their clothing. They would get a $200.00 clothing allowance from the state twice a year. Then we would go by Mikey's work and surprise him on his lunch break and eat lunch with him right by his work at Panera Bread. These were the more "fun" days. Then home, nap, and then off for the afternoon! Finally, at home to rest! Although we didn't rest. It was time to catch up on dishes and laundry and pick up the house. Dinner and repeat routine; bath, play, learn, worship, pray, bed.

Saturday- Mikey worked on Saturdays. He was off Thursdays and Sundays. Saturdays were my day to just kind of relax at home and spend all day with the girls. (Thank God all the Doctor's offices were closed on the weekend! Some reprieve!) We would eat and do crafts and play. Sometimes I'd take them to the mall because they liked going there. Then after Mikey got off work he would play with them outside or we'd use the afternoon to go wash our cars and clean them out with the girls. Or we might go do something fun! Sunday- We would go to church and eat lunch out. Then home to rest (not really) and be together as a family! Also, every single night we had to fill out paperwork for Ann. We had to write down any behavioral problems she had, activities she did, any improvements made, etc. We had to do this for the agency social worker and for the Helen Ross worker. We also had to give both girls their medication(s) every night and log the medicine; when we gave it to them, how many left in the bottle, etc.

Not every week was the same. Some weeks were busier and some weren't as busy. Nevertheless, I always felt like I had a million visits and appointments to do and go to every week. I had to be careful planning future appointments so that I wouldn't make them overlap with another one. The girls had S.T. (speech therapy), P.T. (physical therapy, and O.T. (occupational therapy) every week, and those appointments were at set days and times. The other appointments would vary. Some Doctors they had to see once a week, some once a month, some just once every three months, and then the dentist once every six months. I had to make sure I remembered to call and make the right appointments so the girls would see the right Doctors at the right times, whether it be the once a month Doctors or the once every three months Doctors. Not only did I want to keep up on their appointments, but if I didn't I could get in trouble with the foster care agency and our license could be taken away. I always wanted to do my best in keeping up on their appointments and getting them the help they needed!

The social workers also made me take the girls to the Health Department at least once a year for a complete physical. For some reason, their well check ups at their Doctor didn't "count" for foster kids. They also needed to be examined by the state Health Department. Maybe for a secondary opinion? I don't know. Now, it wasn't always so busy at first. It took time for their developmental problems and behavioral issues to start coming forth. When we first got the girls they were very quiet and to themselves. Once they got to know us, their true selves came out, if you know what I mean. Behavioral issues came out, probably from the anger and frustration of being ripped from their family and not understanding what had gone on. We started noticing developmental issues as they were getting older and couldn't do certain things. The speech was the first apparent setback. Ann had just turned three when we got her and the only word she could say was, "Doi." She couldn't talk at all. She was in speech from the start. But, as time went on, they were referred to more and more specialists and our life got busier and busier.

We didn't mind being busy, because we knew it was for a good cause to help them, but after a while it started wearing on us. Before we knew it our daughter was already turning one year old. Even though we spent as much time with her as we could, the first year of her life flew by. Things started getting more difficult with the girls. At this time, when Alexia turned one in August, Ann also started Kindergarden. I had to take her at 8:00 in the morning and pick her up at 1:00. Mary also started pre-school at Head Start because she had just turned three. I wanted to get her into Head Start to help her to learn and get ahead, instead of behind. I also thought it might help her socially- you know- learn how to play with other kids and make friends. She would go to Head Start from 12:15-4:15. There was a short 45 minute overlap period when Ann and Mary would both be gone at school from 12:15-1:00 and I could have that 45 minute span to just spend alone with my daughter! I thoroughly enjoyed every minute of that time alone with her.

Alexia Jade- One Year Old!

We had so much on our plate that I am surprised we didn't go crazy! Not really. God gave us the peace we needed to get through that two year and seven month period. I was just really thankful that God made me a very organized, administrative (O.C.D... lol) person so that I could handle it all. I always kept appointment cards in my wallet and wrote every appointment on my calendar. I don't think I ever missed any appointment. I was always diligent to make every appointment to get the girls the proper care and help they needed, as exhausting as it was. I made sure I was always on time and even early, too, when I could be. And of course, Mikey was always there to help me whenever he was off work. We did all these things in the midst of learning how to be a parent for the first time to our own new baby girl. God definitely was there for us and with us and gave us enough grace to do everything we needed to!

Okay, so now that the girls were in school, it was even harder to try and do their appointments around their school times since they were opposite. Sometimes I had to take Ann out of school early and sometimes I would have to have Mary miss a day just to get every appointment in for that week. Around this time (after the girls both started school) it started seeming as if that grace to take care of the girls was now leaving us. Mikey and I found ourselves getting frustrated. We also seemed to just keep getting busier and nothing was letting up. And whether it was bad habits from school or jealousy of Alexia or something else, or everything in between, it seemed as if the girls behaviors were getting worse. We loved on the girls and we obviously spent plenty of time with them, but they were still very disobedient, defiant, and stubborn. Ann would lie a lot, too. And now that Ann was in Kindergarden we had to fit in homework every night. We had a hard time doing her homework with her every day. She would never want to do it and would have tantrums and cry and not do it. She would act like she couldn't, but her teacher would tell us that she could do it just fine at school. We didn't know what to do.

CHAPTER TWENTY-THREE

"TO ADOPT, OR NOT TO ADOPT, THAT IS THE QUESTION!"

Mikey and I started questioning if we should still go forward with adopting them. From the day we got them until we found out we were pregnant, all through my pregnancy, delivery, and the whole first year of Alexia's life we always had every intention of adopting them. Now, it was August 2010 and we were starting to question if it was really God's will for us to adopt them. We always pray for God's will to be done. He never told us to adopt them, but we just always wanted to. We also thought it was the right thing to do. God's word says to look after orphans and widows, and in a way they were orphans. We just figured it was God's will, although He never told us specifically to adopt them. So, we seriously started praying for God to really show us if it was His will to adopt them. If it wasn't His will, then we needed to make a choice about what to do. If it was His will, we would hang in there and get through it.

From Alexia's first birthday in August until the Fall, around my birthday in November, we really prayed for God to make it clear. We did not want to give up on these girls and to me it felt like I was giving up on them if we didn't adopt them. I didn't want to let them down or let God down. And we loved them. If we decided not to adopt them, it would be very hard, for us and for them. Like I mentioned earlier, the grace to take care of them was lifting. Mikey and I seemed to be living in frustration from not knowing what else to do with them and for them. It got so bad that we would allow it to get to us and then we would take it out on each other and get mad at each other. We started to not have any peace to adopt them. To make such a big, hard decision we went to our Pastors for prayer and counsel. To be honest, I went there sincerely hoping they would tell me (tell us) to suck it up, hang in there, and not give up on the girls. I thought they would tell us it was God's will for us to adopt them and that we were being selfish by even considering not keeping them. I thought they would pray for us and say it will get better.

To my shock, they said the complete opposite! We told them a little bit about what we were dealing with and our concerns. We told them we were starting to question adopting them. They listened to us and without even hearing everything, they told us they didn't believe we were supposed to adopt them. They said there are two ways to tell when God is not wanting you to do something. They said, "Number one- the grace would lift and number two- you won't have peace." From what we were sharing they could tell the grace God had given us for that time period that He had us take care of them was lifting, and that was a sign that we were done caring for them. Not done with them in a bad way, but the season for them to be with us was ending. They could also tell we didn't have peace anymore to keep them. They advised us to contact the social workers and let them know our decision right away so they could find another adoptive home for them. I left crying and so sad. I guess inside I knew they were right and I didn't want to make that decision.

I didn't want to tell the social workers that we weren't going to adopt them now. We had told them for two and a half years that we wanted to adopt them. I didn't want to be a bad witness to them. I didn't want them to think we were giving up on the girls. God had to remind me it didn't matter what they thought. I didn't need to worry about my reputation. I just needed to obey God and do His will! So, Mikey and I prayed and decided together to make that hard decision. Let me tell you, it was literally the hardest decision that I/we have ever had to make. It was a really tough decision. It was harder to decide not to adopt them than it was to make the decision to move to Tennessee.

I have to interject this right now. At the beginning of October I also found out that I was pregnant with baby number two! We had wanted to have another baby that was about two years apart from Alexia. So, after Alexia's first birthday in August, we tried to get pregnant. It didn't happen. Then we decided to not try in September because we didn't want to have a baby born in June. We have so many family birthdays in June and Father's day and it is so busy that we didn't want to add to the busyness of that month. So, we thought we'd skip September and try again in October for a July baby. Well, I was late for my period and took a pregnancy test at the very end of September and it was negative. I wondered why I was late, but didn't think much about it. Another week went by and I still hadn't started. I tried another pregnancy test and it was positive! Either the first test malfunctioned or I didn't wait long enough to do the test, but I was pregnant! We were ecstatic! After not being able to have kids and then having one we wondered if we would be able to have more. Even though God already gave us a name for a boy and we already had one baby now, our flesh still doubted slightly at times and we wondered if it could happen again. Unfortunately, we all do that at times because of our human nature, but we know deep inside God is faithful to do what He says He will!

The morning I found out I was pregnant was actually the morning we had to go down and meet with the social workers. This was kind of another way I thought maybe our time with the girls was up because I was now pregnant again. It would be very hard for me to take care of all three girls, with all their appointments. That would be a lot for me- more than normal- because of the exhaustion and morning sickness from pregnancy. I would also have to go to all my prenatal appointments now. I thought I was superwomen and could do it still, and I'm sure I could have, but it would have been so hard and taken a toll on my body physically.

Okay, so, Mikey and I typed out a two page letter on our decision and about what and why we were feeling what we were feeling and explained everything to the social workers. We didn't want to just e-mail them or tell them over the phone, so we drove down to Kingsport and I read the letter out loud to them in person. They said they understood, but that they really thought we were doing a great job with the girls and they thought we should still adopt them. We told them thank you, but that our decision was final. We were not going to go back and forth with it. This was mid-November. We wanted them to be able to move the girls to an adoptive home fairly quickly so that they could start bonding with their permanent family.

We were hoping they would move the girls by Christmas. That was still six weeks away and we thought for sure they would find them an adoptive home by then. The reason we wanted them to be moved by Christmas is because we thought that would be a good way for them to bond with their new family- over a fun holiday time. Also, if the family had any other kids, they would have time getting to know them before going back to school in January. We thought it would be a good way to start the new year, in a new home. And because Abby was in school now, it was a great time to switch homes and start Kindergarden at a new school in January after the holiday break, instead of mid-semester. That way she wouldn't be "the new girl" randomly coming in whenever, but she could start back when all the other kids started back.

Now, it was the middle of December and they still hadn't found a home for the girls. We were getting kind of antsy, knowing we had told them our decision a month ago. Since we knew we were not adopting them anymore, we kind of put up our walls and tried not to get further attached to the girls, knowing the more we would get attached the harder it would be for us and for them to leave. I'm sure the girls could feel that pulling away from us, even though we were not intentionally trying to do that. Not only that, but we had planned to go down and stay with my family in Johnson City for three days over Christmas. My Mom did not want the girls to come with us. They did get a little wild, were disruptive, and got into her things, so she didn't want us to bring them. And selfishly, Mikey and I were kind of hoping to have at least this one Christmas to spend with our daughter, alone, before our second child arrived.

We called the social workers to see what was going on and if they had found an adoptive home for them yet. Once you tell a social worker that you are no longer interested in adopting a potential adoptive child, they are supposed to remove the child pretty much immediately and put them in an adoptive home. Since it had been over a month now, we were kind of wondering what was taking so long. They told us that they had a couple homes in mind, but they were trying to wait and see if there was a certain family that would take them after their training had been completed. They said their training would be done in mid-January and that they might possibly be able to move them to that home then.

Knowing we weren't adopting them now and knowing God had showed us that our time with them was finished or "over", we didn't want to drag it out any longer. Our social workers had a hard time at being quick. They procrastinated and drug things out as long as they could. (Maybe not all social workers are like that, but the ones we've been around and had over the years did that.) We told them our concerns for waiting longer and switching Abby's school during it going, instead of at the beginning. We told them my Mom didn't want them at her house and we asked if maybe they could be placed in respite for about four days in a possible adoptive home, during the time we would be at my parents, to see how they would do with the new family. We figured the girls would have more fun at another house anyway, because we weren't big on presents and stuff. We would usually get up on Christmas and pray and read the Bible and then give Alexia and the girls only a few, small gifts. We didn't ever want them to think that Christmas was just about getting presents.

We felt terrible and selfish for doing this around holiday time, but at the same time we knew if we didn't speak up and ask for something, it would be drug out. Besides that, Ann and Mary didn't even really know what Christmas was or when it was, so it's not like they would have an understanding of being left out to go to my family's house for Christmas. To them, it was just another day. They didn't know any different. They were too little to know it was that time of year and what it was about. The social workers didn't think it would be right to send them to another potential adoptive home during Christmas, although we did explain to them that the girls had no understanding of it being Christmas. Because we asked this, they considered it to be a "red flag" and said they had to move the girls immediately now. They found a home for them and picked them up that following Monday on December 21st, right before Christmas.

It was very hard to say bye to them knowing we probably wouldn't ever see them again. Mary didn't really understand what was happening. She didn't even seem sad to leave. I don't think she understood that she wouldn't see us again. Ann was very upset. She was hugging us and not letting go. She was crying. She understood that she was leaving for good. We encouraged her to pray and trust God. We told her to write to us any time. We put our address and pictures in her bag. We encouraged her to be strong and help her sister and to keep watching her worship video. We are thankful to God that she received Jesus into her heart before she left. One day during her worship video she said a prayer to invite Him in her heart. Her and I talked about what that meant and I prayed with her. She loved to worship. I believed and prayed that she would draw closer to Jesus through all of this and all she goes through. He will make her a very strong person. I think Mary was still kind of little to understand the concept of inviting Jesus into her heart, but we know lots of seeds were planted and we believe she will come to know Him some day!

So, they left. They drove away with Ann crying and waving to us and we were crying. We didn't want to sit at home with a really empty house now dwelling on the fact that they were gone. We were having a hard time with it. So, I remember we prayed for them and then we went and saw "Tron" to get our minds off of it. We didn't want Alexia to be too sad, either, so we were trying to get her mind off of it. We had a hard couple days and then we drove down to be with my parents and siblings for Christmas for three days. My family helped us a little and we were comforted by them and they helped us talk it out and get through those feelings of loss that we felt.

CHAPTER TWENTY-FOUR

"OUR SECOND BABY- A BOY!"

After the girls left, it was just me and Alexia at home. Mikey went back to work. Weeks went by and then months and it seemed to get a little easier. We still missed the girls though and we prayed for them diligently. We would send them birthday cards and gift cards and e-mail the social workers to see how they were doing. Alexia did pretty well with the adjustment. I was still a stay-at-home Mom, so I got to spend a little over five months with just her alone, until our second baby arrived on Friday, June 3rd, 2011! I spent a lot of time playing with her, teaching her, and running errands. It was hard enough for me to just have Alexia and run errands while being pregnant again. I had some heart palpitations and was feeling so sick, heavy from the weight gain, and tired towards the end of my pregnancy and I don't know how I would have managed to keep all of the girl's appointments. I was exhausted and my feet swelled bad and I was just ready to get my baby out at like 38 weeks.

To catch you up to this point, I had an ultra sound mid-way through my pregnancy and found out we were having a boy! We were so excited it was a boy! Now, that we already had had three girls, it was so nice to hear that it was a boy! My due date was May 31st, although the midwives changed it to June 9th after an ultra sound. I know it was May 31st, but because he was measuring small on the ultra sound, they pushed it back to June 9th, which is not something a pregnant women wants to hear! Nine more days is a big difference! By May 31st I was ready to have him come out. I was physically miserable. I decided to be induced on June 2nd. That was the earliest they said they could induce me since according to their new due date, that was one week early. They said I would be 39 weeks on the 2nd and that was the earliest to induce. I said okay. According to my calculations, I was already 40 weeks and 2 days on the 2nd. I was ready. So with prayer, Mikey and I decided for me to be induced. I was at a birthing center, not a hospital, so I wanted the baby to come on his own and I wanted it to happen naturally, but I just couldn't wait any longer. I also wanted my family to be there when I was in labor so they could watch Alexia for us. For a few different reasons I won't get into, there were only certain times I knew I could count on my family to be there, so I also picked the 2nd because they could be there then. Also, Alexia's birthday was August 2nd, so I thought it would be neat if his birthday was the same number- June 2nd.

Well, I was induced on June 2nd, with no epidural or pain medication. I still wanted to do it naturally, just like I did with Alexia, with no epidural. I got to the hospital at 6:00 a.m. (I couldn't have the baby at the Birth Center because they won't induce there.) They didn't start inducing me until 8:00 a.m. It took a long time to kick in. I didn't start having contractions until I had 12 mg of Pitocin in my iv. I wouldn't dilate past 4 cm, so we made they choice for the Dr. to break my water around 5:30 p.m. that evening. I thought my baby would never come out. I was nervous they would have to do a C-Section. After my water broke, I finally started progressing about a centimeter an hour. I think around midnight I was finally fully dilated to 10 cm. I was so upset that it was taking so long and upset because I wanted him to be born on June 2nd to have his own birthday. Now it was June 3rd and he would end up sharing a birthday with my sister, Ashley.

I was exhausted by now and super hungry from not eating all day and all night. I felt weak and hopeless. Contractions got worse and I finally started to push. I thought I was going to die. It hurt so bad! My body was shaking and I could barely get the words out to Mikey and my Dad to pray for me. My husband, Dad, and my sister, Ashley, were in the delivery room with me. They were holding my hands, praying for me, and encouraging me! Alexia had fallen asleep in the waiting room with my Mom and other sister. I think I pushed for about 45 minutes before he finally came out. I thought I was going to pass out and that they would have to do a C-Section to get him out. Somehow, by God's grace and my determination, I had the strength to get him out. Our son, Ezekiel Daniel Martinez (we named him just what God told us to name him!), arrived three days after his due date on my sister's birthday at 1:54 a.m. He weighed 7 lbs and 9 oz. He was 20 1/2 inches long. We were so excited to welcome our firstborn son into our lives! Alexia had a playmate again! I was happy he was out and that I was done laboring and everything was okay!

He laid with me all morning and nursed and we bonded greatly and immediately. He ended up having jaundice, too, like Alexia, so I had to put him in the tanning bed! LOL! I tore pretty bad and had to be stitched up. I was in a lot of pain and so we stayed at the hospital until Monday, June 6th. We were there for five days, which felt a little too long. I was ready to go home on Sunday, but we had to wait one more day for me to get better and to see if his jaundice was going away. We went home Monday and had a happy new addition to our family! Alexia did pretty well to the adjustment and we continued with life! I took a long time to heal- about six weeks. I was in a lot of pain for a while and at that time I didn't want to have any more kids because it was such a painful experience. It was also very rough emotionally this time around. They say with each baby it gets easier, but that wasn't true for me this time. It seemed like this time around was a little worse and harder than with my first baby.

Our sweet baby boy, Ezekiel Daniel! One month old.

CHAPTER TWENTY-FIVE

"BACK TO JOHNSON CITY!?"

Ezekiel was born just two months before Alexia turned two. At this time (around Alexia's second birthday) we felt God tell us to leave the church we were attending in Knoxville. We had been there for three and a half years already, but then God said our time there was over. We were going to go one more Sunday to get Ezekiel dedicated because that next Sunday was a baby dedication and we had asked the Pastor(s) to dedicate him to the Lord that day. We were going to have him dedicated and then talk to our Pastor and his wife after the service and tell them we were leaving and what the Lord was showing us. However, the Lord made it clear to it us not to go that next Sunday. He basically said, "I told you it's time to leave. That means this week, don't wait another week." So, we didn't go and we just dedicated him to the Lord ourselves. After leaving that church, the Lord started showing us more insight as to why He had us leave. He showed us some of what was going on spiritually behind the scenes. He also gave me two dreams about the head Pastor/Apostle there and showed me what was happening and had me pray for him. I'm not sure if it would be appropriate to share everything in my book, but let's just say it was a learning experience for me and Mikey. I don't want to leave you with a bad impression of him or anything. He was not in any willful sin or anything like that (that I know of), but the enemy will do anything to get in the midst of people's lives and try to steer them off course.

I will say this though. Witches and warlocks are real. There are people being used by satan to infiltrate the church. Why? To bring deception to God's people and confusion, amongst other things. The Scripture in Matthew 7:15,16a NKJV says, "Beware of false prophets, who come to you in sheep's clothing, but inwardly are ravenous wolves. You will know them by their fruits..." is a very real warning. Why would Jesus warn us and say that if the enemy would never come in to bother the church? These "wolves" dress up as Christians and come in stealth and deceiving. You will never know who they are unless you have discernment from the Holy Spirit. They come off kind and friendly and won't give you any clues that they are working for your enemy. These witches/warlocks like to get involved in kid's ministries, on the prayer team, and on staff to try to lead the congregation, and yes, even the Pastor(s) away. They are very successful when the people and Pastors have a lack of discernment from not walking close to the Spirit or they are blinded by the enemy and/or from their own pride. We have got to be on the look out and be very careful with who we let in our children's ministry and on staff at our churches. If you don't believe witches/warlocks are real, ask God about it.

Let me just tell you that Mikey and I saw first-hand what happens when the enemy is allowed in, without anyone recognizing he is there, and it is awful! We saw our church go from the abiding glory of God's presence, to where people would come to be in the presence of the Lord and worship Him, to just a seeker-friendly typical American church with a set routine and formula to "grow the church". You know, church growth is not just numbers being added to a service. Church growth is when the people that are already there are getting closer to Jesus, leaving sin behind, and living a life of holiness. Church growth is growing in faith and knowing Jesus more intimately. A church is successful when lives are being changed and the presence of God is dwelling there, when it becomes a habitation for the Lord. When a pastor(s) or congregation starts to think that church growth only means that you have to keep adding more people every Sunday, then that is when they become confused to what the goal really is. We knew our Pastor(s) and leaders personally. I really believe they had good intentions and "good hearts" as we say. The Bible says our hearts are evil (Jeremiah 17:9) and that "There is no one who does good, not even one." (Romans 3:12b NIV), but you know what I mean by saying they had good hearts. I just think they were side-swiped by the enemy and fell into his scheme for that church. Mikey and I used to love going there because they just wanted God and wanted to please Him alone. We would have extended worship for like three and a half hours at a time sometimes. They didn't care how late service went. There was no agenda, except to seek God and follow the Spirit as He lead. But unfortunately Mikey and I saw that slip away after about three years.

The church then went from pleasing God to pleasing people. Going from a three or four hour service of all of us experiencing God to a shortened 60 minute routine of worship, announcements, and preaching. It was like God's presence got kicked out and there was no more room for the Spirit. It was so sad and grievous. Any one of us can fall susceptible to the enemy's plans, and that is why we must be on guard and in prayer and in the Word as much as possible!

The next several months, between August and December, we grew much closer to the Lord. He showed us a lot of what was going on in our lives in the spiritual realm. He started revealing what certain Scriptures meant and gave us a deeper understanding of His word. It was a really awesome time! We felt unhindered from hearing Him. At night we would just worship Him and just sit and wait on Him. Sometimes our kids would sit and be with us and sometimes it would be just be me and Mikey after they went to bed. Either way, God was speaking to us! It was one of the best, most refreshing times in our life together so far! Mikey describes this time as "intense." It was so fun, exciting, and we were always expectant to see what God would show us next!

Some nights God would give us a revelation of what a certain verse meant, as we sought Him for wisdom and revelation. Some nights Mikey would see angels. Some nights God would just speak to us and share things with us. One night He gave Mikey some words of encouragement for my Mom. One night Mikey saw three demons walking down our hallway towards us as we were praying. They were coming for a spiritual attack against us. I couldn't see them, but I felt their awful presence. I think our kids saw them as well because they both screamed and pointed at the same time as when I felt them and when Mikey saw them. We prayed and Mikey quoted Scripture and they left. God was teaching us how to fight. We quoted, "No weapon formed against us will prosper," (Isaiah 54:17 NKJV) and "He who is in us is greater than he who is in the world." (1 John 4:4 NIV) And we told them to leave in Jesus's name. It was a little scary, I'm not going to lie, but they left and God was right there with us, teaching us.

God was also teaching us how to clean out our house physically because physical things in our house affect us spiritually. We got rid of everything that offended God, our Father, including some shirts, two pinatas we had saved, movies, and toys. He had showed me some things about Disney and Disneyland, also, during this time. He gave me insight into what Disneyland is all about and the evil there. We got rid of Disney things that we had in our house, which wasn't much, but we did have a few "Disney" items. One night we just went around the whole house and prayed in each room and asked Him to show us what offended Him or displeased Him and we threw it away. Mikey and I would both feel confirmation about each thing He showed us and we were in unity. We went downstairs and were in front of our bookshelf with some movies on it. We barely had any movies anyway because we are not big movie people, but there were three specific movies the Lord told us to get rid of, and He told us why. In case you are wondering which movies they were, here you go: "Shrek", "Napoleon Dynamite", and "Enchanted". He told us "Shrek" because it had a "Spirit of perversion" attached to it. He told us "Napoleon" because it had a "Deaf and dumb Spirit" behind it. He told us "Enchanted" because He said it had "Spirits of witchcraft, magic, and sorcery" in it, which is detestable to Him.

I know we can all see those things (perversion, dumbness, magic, etc.) interwoven in those movies, but God was showing us that there were actual "Spirits" (a.k.a. demons) attached to those movies and when we allowed ourselves to watch those movies it would open the door in our own spirits for those demons to come on in! I don't mean come in to possess us or anything like that, but I mean they would be allowed in our physical house and they would be given access to mess with us! Isn't that something to think about?! Not only would we open the door for the enemy to bother us, but God didn't like us watching things like that. It dishonored Him, as His Word says to be careful what we fix our eyes upon. It kind of gives a whole new reality to the Scriptures in Matthew 6:22, 23 NKJV "The eye is the lamp of the body; so then if your eye is clear, your whole body will be full of light. But if your eye is bad, your whole body will be full of darkness. If then the light that is in you is darkness, how great is the darkness!" If something is detestable to God, we should obviously not partake in it, but we should also not put it before our eyes. By watching what is detestable to Him, our spirits are still partaking in it. So, we took the movies outside to break them and throw them in our outside trash. They wouldn't break at first! Once Mikey finally broke them, he noticed that there were two discs from each movie. One for the movie and one for the subliminal messages in the movie. I won't get in to "subliminal messaging" right now, but it is real. Ask the Lord about it and research it! So, anyway, we got rid of a lot of stuff!

One of the things God told us during this time is, "It's time to sell your house." This was in November of 2011. So, we put it up for sale ourselves on Craigslist and nothing happened. So, then we hired a realtor. He put it up for sale, took pictures, did open houses, etc. and it still wasn't selling. God didn't say where to go next, so we kept seeking Him and He then told us He wanted us to move back to Johnson City. We said okay, even though we really didn't want to go back there. We really liked Knoxville. Then we prayed about what job Mikey would get when we would go back. There was a bread route open in Johnson City that one of Mikey's friends from Food City told him about. He was a bread vendor in Knoxville, but he knew there was an opening in Johnson City. It would give Mikey plenty of hours and a much higher pay. He applied for it.

After a lot of prayer and several confirmations, he got the job! When God tells you to do something, He always makes a way for it to happen! Mikey was going to start right after New Years of 2012. He put his two weeks notice in at Food City. We didn't know exactly where to move to yet, and since our house was up for sale, we couldn't afford to buy something in Johnson City, too. It would be really hard to even rent an apartment. We couldn't afford to keep making our house payment (until it sold) and pay rent for another place. So, we moved into my parent's downstairs bonus room/finished basement until we knew what was going on and where God wanted us to live. We only lived there with them for three months. During this time Mikey worked the bread job faithfully, even in the snow! He worked from 3:30 a.m. till 12:30 p.m. (lunch time).

Although it was nice for me and the kids because my hubby and their Daddy got to be home by lunch time every day, it wasn't so nice for Mikey because when he did get home he was exhausted. He would eat with us and play with the kids, but by 7:00 p.m. he was ready for bed. He would go to bed by 7:00 or 8:00 to be able to get enough sleep for the job. It was physically rough. He had a specific time period for training. He was allotted three months to train and try the job and then he had to make a decision to do this for sure/full time/ permanently and buy his route or opt out of it altogether. Even though three months went by, his body was still not adjusting to this schedule.

One morning Mikey got up like normal and got ready for work. He got up to the front door and was about to leave and he had an erie feeling and God told him, "Don't go out the front door." He came back down the stairs, not knowing exactly what was going on, but obeying the Lord anyway. At the bottom of the stairs was the door to the bonus room and on the other side of the bonus room was our bedroom. The exact same time Mikey entered the bonus room from one side, I opened the bedroom door and entered the bonus room from the other side. We met each other in the middle, in the bonus room, to share with one another what we each just experienced. I was just woken up by a vivid, scary dream from the Lord. It was a dream of warning and God was showing me what was going on outside spiritually. In my dream I saw lots of dogs all over my parent's grass and front yard. They were all scary looking dogs, almost like ferocious wolves, and they were all facing the front door. I knew they represented demons. There was more to the dream, which I won't get in to, but let's just say I knew Mikey wasn't supposed to go out the door and go to work that day.

I just want to throw in something here. Even though Jesus lives in us and "He who is in us is greater than he that is in the world," we must also use wisdom. If God is saying, "Don't go out the door," we can't say, "Oh, I'll be fine. I'm covered in the blood." That may be true, but when we are disobedient to God, and not following His will, we are on our own, without His protection. I believe we come out from under His covering. Just like in the Bible, when God's people weren't obedient He removed His protection from them and they were taken by the enemy physically and spiritually. I have had Christians tell me I don't need to fear evil and God's protecting me, etc., and that's true, but they aren't balancing it with being in His will. If Mikey went out the door that day and something bad happened to him, it would not be God's fault. We couldn't blame God for not protecting us. We could only blame ourselves for not being obedient and for not listening to His voice!

Chapter Twenty-Six

"FACEBOOK INTERJECTION"

While I'm talking about this, I want to talk about Facebook for a minute. During this season, from about October 2011 until March of 2012, there were specific topics and things I felt lead by the Lord to share specifically on Facebook. Trust me, I didn't "want to go there" with certain topics, but when the Lord prompts me to do something, I must be obedient. I will be accountable for not saying something when I should of. James 4:17 NKJV says, "Therefore, to him who knows to do good and does not do [it], to him it is sin." So, when I felt God put on my heart certain things He wanted me to share; to warn, exhort, and encourage His people with, then I had to do it. There were also subjects that were on the Lord's heart that He wanted to share with me. He wanted me to be a voice and share with the rest of the body that I had contact with. Some things were things that were bothering Him that His children were doing or allowing that weren't pleasing to Him. When His children read my posts on Facebook they became accountable for what they read and heard.

I know a lot of people on Facebook, especially Christians, did not like what I shared, but it didn't matter. God let whoever needed to read it, read it. It was everyone's choice as to what their response was. If they got mad and offended and accused me of being judgmental or if they considered what was said and took it to the Lord in prayer- either way, that was between them and God. Galatians 1:10 HCSB says, "For am I now trying to win the favor of people, or God? Or am I striving to please people? If I were still striving to please people, I would not be a servant of Christ." That is exactly how I felt during that time. I am here to know God, Jesus, and Holy Spirit, and to do what He asks me to do. I am not here to win favor from Facebook "friends" by posting sugar-coated messages. I spoke raw truth from God's word and I showed love to my fellow believers by being bold enough to do so, in hopes that it would help them to see truth and be "set free".

During that time I lost many "friends" that didn't like how I said things. Instead of looking at the truth in the message, they judged me on how I said it. I came against some opposition in the physical and spiritual realm in that season. I had to fight not to be discouraged and not give up with what God was having me do. On a more positive side, there was also a lot of good that came from it. I got a lot of private messages saying thank you for being bold and sharing what needed to be shared. Other people felt the same way as me, but were afraid to say anything or post anything. They were grateful I spoke up. Others were encouraged in the Lord and others just needed to hear what was written at that time. So, amongst opposition came encouragement and support for me from sincere believers as well. Just like in the New Testament- the disciples came against tremendous opposition, but yet God was still blessing them and using them to bring people to Him and to divide the people by His truth. The biggest opposition came from the Pharisees, just as now the biggest opposition to those truly following Jesus comes from the church, religious spirits, and other believers. From my experience non-believers seem to praise true believers and want what they have, while other believers and church members just want to judge you for speaking the truth boldly.

After this time I still kept posting things here and there, but it was not as intense as it was for that season. Eventually, I think at the end of 2012 or beginning or 2013, the Lord pretty much told me I was "done" sharing and that my time was up for Facebook. Not that I couldn't ever go on Facebook again, but that my time for testifying on there and sharing intense posts about certain topics was over. I said what needed to be said and I could see people's hearts getting hard and not wanting to hear the truth anymore. It reminded me of the Scripture that says, "For a time is coming when people will no longer listen to sound and wholesome teaching. They will follow their own desires and will look for teachers who will tell them whatever their itching ears want to hear." (2 Timothy 4:3 NLT). In March of 2013 I deactivated my Facebook altogether and took a break. Besides posting what God lead me to, I also liked posting pictures and personal updates, but that was so time consuming! So, I wanted a break.

CHAPTER TWENTY SEVEN
"BACK TO MY STORY"

Wow, long rabbit trail! Okay, so what I was saying is that Mikey needed to be obedient and not go to work or else He wouldn't be in the protection of God's will. What lead me to think about Facebook and go off on that bunny trail is because of this idea that we are protected no matter what. I had posted a long post about Disneyland on Facebook one time. The Lord had showed me a lot of insight about Disneyland during this same season of Facebook posting time. I posted what He showed me in hopes that other believers would see how the enemy works through supposed fun and harmless places. It is a long post and a lot to go into, but the main thing God showed me/told me was that He didn't want me and my family to go to Disneyland. (Not just to me, but He showed Mikey, too.) Because the Lord showed me this and I posted it, a lot of Christians took offense because they liked Disneyland. I never said anyone should avoid it, I just shared what God showed me.

An old friend of mine, actually a couple of old friends, took my post as if I was afraid of what was harmful there spiritually. They would say things in ignorance not knowing what they were saying. One lady told me, "I don't need to be afraid to go there, I'm covered by the blood." That's great she's covered in the blood, but she doesn't fully understand how God's protection works. (I don't think any of us understand it fully yet, but if He shows us more insight into it, we need to listen.) If the Lord told me something specific like, "Don't go to Disneyland," then I need to listen and not go. It has nothing to do with being covered in the blood. It has to do with being obedient because I want to please the Lord. There is a spirit of death that resides at Disneyland. People have died there, while in the park, physically. Yes, God is well able to protect me from the spirit if death, of course, but if I go out of disobedience, God is not obligated to protect me anymore. If something were to happen to me, it would be my own fault. I could only blame myself. We must use wisdom and not be ignorant of the devil's vices. We must also not ignore God's wisdom and direction.

So, this morning when God showed both Mikey and I separately for Mikey not to leave, he needed to listen and obey God, and he did. He called his boss and told him the truth of why he was not coming in to work. Mikey wasn't embarrassed and didn't make up an excuse, he simply told his boss what God showed him and told him my dream. His boss said, "okay." He listened to everything Mikey shared and he said it changed him. Mikey had already been witnessing to him for the last three months while training with him, so he knew what kind of people Mikey and I were. He knew we obeyed God and that Mikey wouldn't come in if that's what God showed him.

This same morning we stayed up and prayed and asked God to show us His will. Did He want Mikey to stay at this job or was he just there for a season to learn more things spiritually and to witness to this guy? He made it clear to us for Mikey not to buy the route. His time was up and he opted out. So, now we were just praying for the "what next?" I won't get into this, but we weren't really having a good time being at my parent's house. Once you have your own family, it is hard to live under your Mom and Dad again. Any of you who have had to live with your parents after being married know what I am talking about! We didn't want to stay with my parents anymore and now Mikey was out of a job. We didn't think we could get an apartment to rent. We didn't want our house in Knoxville to go into foreclosure. We decided to go back to Knoxville and move back into our house.

Chapter Twenty-Eight

"BIG MISTAKE"

So, we moved back into our house in Knoxville and Mikey was able to be re-hired at Food City. He did a good job there and they liked him, so they hired him back. When in Johnson City (before we moved back) I had someone tell me that this same scenario happened to someone in their family. They put their house up for sale. Then they moved and got a new job in a different city. It didn't work out. They moved back into their home because it didn't sell. I thought maybe that's what God wanted us to do. Maybe this lady told me that for a reason. Maybe He was just testing us to see if we would really put our house up for sale and really move. Then He would say we passed the test and we could go back to our house in Knoxville. We weren't sure. We didn't hear Him tell us anything, so we went back. That was a mistake. We didn't wait on the Lord long enough and we took matters into our own hands-never a good idea!

We moved back right after Resurrection Sunday in 2012. I think it was the very end of March or beginning of April. Mikey went back to work and the kids and I unpacked and went back to our normal routine. It was nice to be back in our own home. We had Ezekiel's first birthday at our house. We had a fantastic and fun Summer, just the four of us as a family. We went to the water parks, the Lake, took a really inexpensive two day vacation to Pigeon Forge, etc. It was a great Summer, but Mikey and I were still feeling like we were missing something. We starting feeling uneasy and not peaceful. We were feeling "out of place." We, of course, were praying for God's will. One day, while Mikey was feeling all of this, he went out to mow. While he was mowing, he prayed and asked God, "Why are we back here again in Knoxville?" God answered him.

He said, "You moved back out of fear. You didn't trust Me. Now, you are going to have to trust Me more than you have ever had to before." Mikey noticed that as he mowed, some spots were easy because it was flatter and the grass was easy to cut. Some spots were harder because it was uphill and the grass was thicker and harder to cut. God said, "This is how this walk is. Sometimes it's easy, sometimes it gets hard, but you must go up the hill and trust Me." Then He reminded Mikey that He told us to sell our house. He also reminded Mikey that He originally moved us to Johnson City from California. He said, "I want you back where I originally moved you to." Knoxville was just a season for training- not permanent. He also told Mikey to go read Jonah. You know the story. God gave him a second chance.

Before this, I had also felt led to read and study the book of Jonah. God always makes it clear when He shows us something. I think I saw the book of Jonah three times in about a weeks period. Mikey and I saw a children's Jonah book at the hospital when we had to go there to check Ezekiel's head from falling. Then we saw two different Jonah books at other places. We were like, "Okay, God, we get it." LOL! He wanted us to read it for many reasons, but I think mainly to show us that He was giving us a second chance to go back to Johnson City again and obey Him. Of course we repented and took the second chance gratefully! One of the cool things about God is that He is so loving and gracious. When He told Mikey we moved back out of fear and didn't trust Him, it was so encouraging to just hear from God again. It was not condemning or rude. His presence just filled us and we still felt His love for us despite our mistake. This was a real mistake, not willful sin. We really thought we were in His will, but since He hadn't told us to go back to Knoxville, we weren't in His will. We felt awful for not being in His will, but we also felt hopeful because we knew He would turn this situation into something redemptive.

So, we started packing again! We started to look for places to rent in Johnson City. Long story short- I had had a dream about an electrical van with Mikey's old boss's company name on it from Johnson City. I told Mikey and we prayed about the dream and for a job for Mikey. We both knew it was God's will for Mikey to go back and work for that same company again- Marty's Electric. There was more for Mikey to learn doing electrical work for what God has planned for us in the future. Mikey talked to Marty and we drove down so Mikey could meet with him. He hired Mikey back after four years of being gone in Knoxville! He also gave Mikey the amount of pay we needed now so I could still stay home and take care of the kids! We were very thankful! We also found an inexpensive townhouse for rent between my parent's house and Mikey's boss's house. With much prayer, we were accepted and got the town house! Before we moved, like I mentioned, we got to celebrate Ezekiel's first birthday in our house and also Alexia's third birthday! Here is a picture of him at on year old!

Ezekiel Daniel- One Year Old!

God was also speaking to us again during the time we were packing and getting ready to move back to J.C. He gave me the Scripture in Acts to, "Sell all you have and give to the poor." Mikey and I put our "stuff" on Craigslist for sale and sold what we could. We sold cribs, end tables, a couch, lamps, etc. I think God was helping us make it easier to move! LOL! He also wanted us to realize our security is not in our stuff, no matter how nice it may have been; our security is In Him, not our things! We didn't need all the stuff we had. So, we sold our stuff, Mikey put his notice in at Food City, again, and we moved to Johnson City as soon as we could. The fastest Mikey could start work and the fastest we could get the townhouse was September 8th, so we moved! We liked our townhouse. We moved on a Saturday and Mikey started work that Monday after two days of unpacking. The kids and I had to adjust to our new place and new schedule, with Mikey getting home at 4:30 now, instead of 2:30. It took a little getting used to, but we were okay!

CHAPTER TWENTY-NINE

"WHY ARE WE CELEBRATING CHRISTMAS?!"

So, it was now a few months later and we were at the end of 2012. We were back in Johnson City, Mikey was doing electrical work again, and we were seeking the Lord. You know, this walk with Christ is not always easy. It is sometimes lonely and difficult standing for what you believe, especially when your friends and family don't stand with you. Christmas just passed and it is now December 28th, 2012. Mikey and I were convicted somewhat last year about celebrating Christmas, so we started researching "Christmas", its origin, and what it means to celebrate it now. We learned that it started as a pagan holiday, or "holy day", called "Winter Solstice". The pagans would celebrate and worship their god(s), especially their god, "Saturnalia" on December 25th to bring in the Winter cycle or "Winter Solstice". They would cut down a tree and decorate it (Jeremiah 10:3,4) and give each other gifts. Later, when Christianity started spreading in Rome, the people did not want to get rid of their "holiday." They didn't want the Christians to make them stop celebrating that day. So, what they did was Christianize the holiday. They put a mask over what they were really doing. The Romans started calling this holiday "Christ's Mass" instead of "Winter Solstice." They told the Christians they were celebrating Christ's birth. So, needless to say, they tricked the Christians and the Christians got sucked into celebrating this pagan holiday with the pagans, not understanding its true intent. Christians thought they were celebrating Jesus, when in fact they were just participating in an occult ritual with worship to false gods. The true meaning of this "holiday" is to worship false gods, not Jesus, and it is still the same today.

According to the Bible, Jesus's birth day was on or around the Feast of Tabernacles, which would put his birthday at the end of September or beginning of October. That should truly give us a clue right there. If we were really celebrating his birthday, we would celebrate it at the proper time, in the Fall, late September/early October, not in December? And also, if God wanted us to know Jesus's true date of earthly birth, He would have told us. I think God wants it to remain a mystery so no one will celebrate his birthday or make an idol out of that day. God is eternal- Jesus has no beginning and no end, so celebrating His earthly entrance is kind of futile, in my opinion. We should always celebrate His omniscience and His "without beginning or end" being.

In learning all of this, and by what God was revealing to us through His spirit, we felt God wanted Mikey and I to give up celebrating "Christmas" as it dishonors Him and does not please Him or bring Him glory. In doing so, we have had other Christians judge us for it and say things like, "You're legalistic," and "Do you think you're better than everyone else?" Sometimes giving up things that even the "Christian" world finds acceptable is not easy, but it is worth it to please the King! That finds us lonely at times and feeling like we are so alone in this world. Often, Mikey and I feel like we are the only ones left that truly are different and have a different mindset than the majority of the church. I feel like Elijah. God, am I the only one? He says, "No, I have others." By saying I/we feel that way does not mean we are better than anyone. It just means we have a hard time finding people like us that are like-minded and believe what we believe and share in the same things we share in.

When we share with our family or other Christians the things God has shown us and done for us, or the things we've given up for Him, the usual response is that of a deer in headlights! They don't know what to say or think in response to what we've told them. It is definitely awkward at times. Occasionally, we have some people say, "That's awesome, God's been showing me the same thing." Those kind of responses encourage us! Giving up a fun holiday is just one of the ways we show Jesus that we love Him more than that holiday. We love Him more than Christmas. If we did not love Him more than Christmas, then we wouldn't give it up. Jesus said to him, "You shall love the LORD your God with all your heart, with all your soul, and with all your mind." Matthew 22:37 NKJV.

We are not going to condemn anyone we meet that still celebrates Christmas- that is between them and God. This book is my testimony and what God has shown me and what I have chosen to do in response to what He has shown me. Also, one more side note about the actual "Christmas tree". A friend of ours told us a verse in the old testament, in Jeremiah 10:3,4 NIV that says, "For the customs (traditions) of the people are worthless. Someone cuts down a tree from the forrest; it is worked by the hands of a craftsman with a chisel. 4 He decorates it with silver and gold. It is fastened with hammer and nails, so it won't totter." If that does not sound like the description of a Christmas tree, then I don't know what does. To me (and Mikey), when we heard that Scripture, it was very clear to us to not have a "Christmas tree" in our home any more, and we told our friend thank you for pointing that out to us.

Just recently, I was reading Deuteronomy and I came across the part where Moses is telling God's people what to do and not do when they cross into the Jordan. He tells them, from the Lord, to "Not follow the way of the people's custom of how they worship". (Read Jeremiah 10 and the book of Deuteronomy for more understanding) He was not just telling them not to worship their "gods," but not even to imitate the way they worshipped their gods. Whatever way(s) the pagan people chose to worship, God didn't even want the Israelites to learn or follow their ways of worship, even if they were "worshipping Him" and not the false gods. He tells them to not worship how or where they worshipped. He told them to only worship Him in the place He chose and the way He chose and laid out for them to worship. That is something to stop and think about right there!

As I was thinking about what I read as I was going to sleep that night, Christmas came to my mind again. It was the way of the pagans to cut down trees from the forrest, decorate them with silver and gold and make them steady with fastened nails. That sounds just like what we do today. People cut down pine trees and bring them to Christmas tree lots and then we purchase them. Then we decorate them with precious ornaments (some of which are silver and gold) and we fasten it tight with nails or those handy plastic stands with the fasteners. If that doesn't sound like we are copying the way of the pagans, then I don't know what does! We, as Christians, say we are "worshipping" the Lord by having a Christmas tree in our house, or that it reminds us of Him or the cross. Can I just venture to say that God hates it? If He didn't like His people copying the ways of "worship" from the pagans back then, then why would He like His people doing the same thing now? His word says, "He is the same yesterday, today, and forever." He doesn't change. If He hated it then, He hates it now!

I've heard Christians, and even my own family, tell me that their Christmas tree is not an idol. Okay, so maybe the tree is not an idol. Having an idol or copying the way of the pagans is two separate issues, but they are both still "bad" and God doesn't like either. I want to ask you the same question that Mikey and I asked ourselves: "What is the point of having a Christmas tree in my/our house?" I couldn't come up with a reason. I didn't know why we always had one every year. It was just a custom and a tradition I had always known, so we continued it after we got married. "You have let go of the commands of God and are holding on to human traditions," Mark 7:8 NIV. This is what Mikey and I were doing. We were holding onto traditions, without even knowing why we were holding onto them and without asking the Holy Spirit what He thought about it. We thought it was about time we asked Him what He thought about it.

In conclusion, I am going to dare to say that I believe the "Christmas tree" is, in fact, an idol. Whether we bow down to it or not is not necessarily what makes it an idol. I think it is an idol and I'll tell you why. Where do most of us put our tree? Usually in the living room. What do we do with a Christmas tree? We adorn it as if it were something special or worth value, like we do as we adorn Jesus with our worship. What is the focal point of our living room for the average of one month out of every year? Our Christmas tree. It is where our eyes go and where our attention is the whole time that it is in our house. And on Christmas morning, where does everyone sit? Around the tree. We also spend lots of money to put pretty ornaments on it and on the presents we put under it. If that does not sound like modern day idolatry, then I don't know what does.

I've heard Christians say that having their Christmas tree is supposed to be a reminder of the cross because it is a tree, and trees are made out of wood, and the cross was made out of wood. Okay, but I thought at Christmas we were celebrating His birth, not death? If it reminds you of His cross and death, then why not have it up on "Easter", not Christmas? Personally, seeing a decorated Christmas tree does not remind me of the cross, but of all the presents I will get on Christmas morning! Let's be real here LOL! And to mention presents real quick, how are we worshiping God by giving each other gifts and not Him? If we had a party to celebrate my birthday and all my family and friends came (three months late, as we celebrate His birthday three months late) and then gave each other gifts and no one brought anything for me, how do you think I would feel? If no one brought presents for me, only for themselves, wouldn't that be a little dishonoring to me? I am just very passionate about it now because I always want to please Him, honor Him with the choices I make, and then encourage other believers to do the same.

I don't mean to turn this book into a sermon of me preaching about why we shouldn't celebrate Christmas, but it is part of my testimony. It is a part of what God has shown me (and my husband) and I am sharing it because it has changed me. I'm passionate about this subject now. If this bears witness to you, then praise God! If you are still not convinced or don't think I am right by what I am sharing with you, then go to God and talk to Him about it. Ask Him to show you the truth about Christmas and ask Him if it pleases Him. If you want to keep celebrating it and you don't care if it pleases Him or not, then disregard everything I just shared with you. You have your own free will and your own choice.

Chapter Thirty

"WALKING OUT LOVE"

God has been so faithful to show His love to me. One of the ways He has shown His love to me is through my husband. He has shown me how to love and forgive like nobody else has before. He walks it out, not just says it. Just recently he displayed a perfect example of what walking out love looks like. He was on the phone with someone, a family member, having a conversation with him. In an instant the phone call went sour and I witnessed my husband being insulted, accused falsely, he was getting yelled at, being put-down, belittled, etc. This person on the other end was exasperating him. My husband had done nothing wrong, and even if he had done something wrong, it would have been a mistake out of a clear conscience. My husband had no wrong motives and no intention to hurt this person. This person was just so full of anger and hatred himself, that he didn't know how to communicate with love and talk out a miscommunication.

I watched as my husband sat there patiently, trying to lovingly apologize for anything he did wrong. I am his witness that he did absolutely nothing wrong, but to make peace and walk in humility, he humbled himself and said he was sorry for any miscommunication and sorry for arguing. He had not even argued, but this person insisted he was arguing. He apologized anyway. There was no way he could argue when the conversation was one-sided. My husband put the phone on speaker and I continued to hear this person blame my husband for something that only this other person could take responsibility for. He blamed Mikey, tried to condemn him and even threw out that, "You're going to answer to God for this..." manipulation. I sat there nervously praying for my husband to not receive the lies being thrown at him by the enemy. I prayed for God to give him wisdom in that moment. I prayed for God to give him boldness to say what needed to be said out of love.

After these few minutes (that seemed like such a long time) passed; insult after accusation, belittlement after condemnation, this person finally hung up on Mikey after he yelled what he needed to say and I waited to see what my husband's reaction would be. With tears flowing down his face and a broken heart from feeling so hurt from someone so close to him, he said, "I still love him and I forgive him. God, please forgive him because he doesn't even know what he is doing. He doesn't realize how bad he hurts me, or maybe he does, but either way, please forgive him. I forgive him." Now, after Mikey said that I was sitting there on the floor crying, too, feeling upset and so angry with this person for not seeing my husband for who he really is, but at the same time feeling so happy and blessed to see what a godly, mature husband I have.

I think what I was most upset about was the fact that if this person truly took the time to know Mikey and saw him for who God sees him as, and not how he had seen him in the past, before he started serving the Lord, then he would know Mikey would never intend to hurt him or do anything wrong to him. In fact, he would do everything he could to please him and make him happy and proud of him. That is why I get angry. I just wanted to text this person or e-mail him and tell him Mikey did nothing wrong. I wanted to bring justice to the situation. I wanted to tell him Proverbs 18:13 NKJV that says, "He who answers a matter before he hears [it], it [is] folly and shame to him." I wanted to tell him that Mikey didn't do anything wrong and that he should learn how to be quiet at some point and let Mikey explain. I wanted this person to see that we are living for God and abiding in His will and that he was wrong for saying the things he said. Mikey said, "No, you don't need to do that. You don't need to defend me or us. You just need to forgive him."

I'm like, "Wow, okay." Easier said than done, but it is a choice to forgive, not a feeling or emotion. We, as Christians, must forgive. We have to, we're commanded to. Colossians 3:13 NKJV says, "Bearing with one another, and forgiving one another, if anyone has a complaint against another; even as Christ forgave you, so you also must do. That is walking out love. Forgiving is walking out love. I got to see my husband truly walk out love! So, I forgave, too. When we try to defend ourselves, it is because we still have pride in us and we are worried about our reputation. When we don't try to defend ourselves, and we pray for the offender instead, then Jesus can defend us and we be free from that burden. Jesus never defended Himself. He knew who He was. When we know who we are in Christ, it is easy to forgive and move on, without feeling the need to prove ourselves to anyone. Again, easier said than done, but it takes one little choice at a time.

Chapter Thirty-One

"OUR NEW PLACE"

A couple of weeks after that incident I had a dream that we moved again. We moved into a one-story house. The dream got me to start thinking about moving again. Our six month lease we signed at our current townhouse was almost up and we didn't know if we should stay there for another six months or move. We had been praying for God to lead us. We didn't really want to move again. After all, it is a lot of work and it costs money to move. We would rather have stayed at our town house, but we wanted to be in God's will. Because of my dream, I started looking online for apartments, town houses, and homes for rent. Since I had that dream about moving again, it could be God speaking to me and showing me that we are to move again, so looking for some new place wouldn't hurt. We found one in our price range that looked nice from the pictures. I scheduled an appointment to see it. There were a couple minor things we didn't like, but overall it was nice and we liked it.

To back up a bit, Mikey and I talked about moving after I had this dream and also because our lease was just about up. We decided if we moved it would definitely be in Johnson City, not Jonesborough (which is where our townhouse currently was- on the outskirts of Johnson City), and we also decided we wanted something cheaper. We wanted a place that was less expensive and with water included so we could save money every month. We were barely making it by every month in the townhouse we were in so we decided it would be wisdom to get something more inexpensive. When Mikey and I talked, I said, "This is wise for us to move. We can save money on rent and have one less bill if we find a place with water included."

You know sometimes God leads us directly through wisdom. What I mean by that is even if God didn't speak to us directly and lead us specifically to move, He still gives us wisdom to make the best choice. Sometimes God doesn't give us every answer all up front with all the details, but He will lead us through wisdom and peace. Even though our flesh might want a nice house that is big so we can show it off to our friends and family, if it is going to cause us to get behind or get in debt, then it is probably safe to say it is not God. We can look in the Bible and see it is not God because it doesn't line up with Scripture. Getting a smaller, inexpensive place that we can afford and save money is wisdom. So, it would be in God's will for us to use wisdom and not be in debt. Yes, it might be hard to downsize. It might be an adjustment to make to get a smaller apartment, instead of a townhouse, but that is where we can choose to walk in God's will and in wisdom, or walk in our flesh. We could have felt embarrassed to live in an apartment. What would our friends think if we live in an apartment and not a nice house? It doesn't matter what anyone thinks, but it matters what God thinks. Being in His will and walking in wisdom is far better than showing off a house to friends and family. When we are in His will, is when we are in peace.

So, that night I was praying and waiting on the Lord. I asked Him if this was the right place for us. All I heard him speak to me was, "What was the lady's name that showed you the house?" I said, "Shannon." He said, "Go look up what her name means. You'll find the answer in her name." So, I was like, "Okay." I was already in bed and didn't know where my name book was at that moment, so I decided to go to bed and look it up first thing in the morning. That same night, I woke up at some point during the night and I heard the Lord say, "Just as I am giving you a new physical roof over your head, I am also giving you a new spiritual roof over your head; a new protection." I was like, "Sweet! Thank you." And I fell back to sleep. (Not only was that a cool, encouraging word from the Lord, but He also confirmed for us to move! Double bonus!)

The next morning I woke up and found my name book right away. I looked up the name "Shannon" and here's what it said, "Wise" and "Inspired of God." Now, you have to know something about the Lord. This doesn't mean He was saying, "Yes" to that particular place we looked at, but He was leading us and showing us that we were in the right direction. Now, before in our immaturity, we would have taken this answer from the name book as Him saying, "Yes, take that particular place." Now, as we have grown more and know God a little more than we did before, we know He is just saying to us, through this answer, "You are in the right direction. You are being "wise" by moving into Johnson City. You are being "wise" to find something cheaper, with water included. You are on the right path and this move is indeed "Inspired of Me." Isn't that cool that He used someone's name and what it means to speak to us and confirm something to us?! He can use anything, including a donkey and a rock!

With that peace in our hearts now, knowing God is in fact leading us to move, and with the confirmation of what "Shannon" means, we were happy to keep looking for a new place! We looked at about 10 different places. They just didn't seem to be the "right one". There were a couple we liked, but they didn't have a washer or they were too far or there was just something we didn't quite like or feel peace about. I found a brand new apartment on Craigslist and it seemed too good to be true. It was only $591.00 a month for a two bedroom, two bathroom apartment. It was brand new, with new carpet and a refrigerator and washer and dryer! We inquired about it, but never saw it. We were still trying to look for something cheaper, closer to $550.00. We saw the outside of these apartments one day while driving home from another place we looked at. I didn't remember the name and didn't realize this was the same one I read about on Craigslist. I told Mikey I would call and ask about it, but it looked like it would be way too nice and way too expensive for us. It was so nice and I wished we could move there!

So, I called and found out it was the same one on Craigslist. So, we eventually came and looked at it. We were astounded at how nice and big these apartments were! They had huge bedrooms, walk in closets, and new everything! No one had lived in them, yet. They were gorgeous and immaculate! We filled out a very long application and gave them a deposit to hold one for us and our application fees. Then we prayed! They said they would get back to us in about a week to a week and a half to let us know if we were approved or not. I called after that time had passed to check on our applications because we had still not heard anything back. They said they still didn't know yet or have our results yet. We kind of needed to know quickly because our lease was about to be up at our current place and we needed to find somewhere to move quick! If not this place, then we needed to get something else soon!

After three weeks of waiting, I was beginning to get irritated that these people were not getting back to us. It was now Wednesday, March 13th and our lease was going to be up in two days on Friday, March 15th! Two days left until we have to move out of our current townhouse. I was driving to Wal*Mart, with my Mom and sister driving behind me. They were coming to help me pick up the kid's toddler beds we ordered for them. I wasn't at peace and was feeling anxious, so I turned up my worship music to worship Jesus. I prayed and invited Him in the car and asked for His presence to be with me and for peace. I immediately felt His presence and calmed down. I then pulled into Wal*Mart and a car turned and pulled in front of me and the license plate read "777"! That is how I know God is with me and leading me. It is a confirmation that *I am* on the right path! He speaks to me quite often through the number "777". The number seven is the number for perfection and completeness. Three sevens in a row means it is a sure thing and will be done and confirms we are headed in the right direction!

So, seeing the "777" on the license plate is no coincidence to me, especially after I just prayed for His presence to come and for His will to be done and then I saw it immediately after. So, we finished shopping, ran some errands and decided to go by the apartments to check on our application in person. On the way there, right before we got to the apartments, I saw a different car parked on the side of the road in a random place that also said "777" on the license plate! I smiled and said to myself, "Okay, God, I trust You, and I know we will get this apartment. Help me be patient and trust You." We arrived and went in there to inquire about the application and they said they hadn't heard back from "compliance" yet and they would call us when they know. We reminded them we needed to be out of our place in two days if they could please check on it.

We left and about two hours later they called my Mom's cell phone. I gave them her number because I did not not have a cell phone. She pulled off the road in front of me and flagged me down. She got out of her car and ran to my window to let me know they called and that we were approved! I was nervous seeing her on the side of the road. I thought something bad happened or their car broke down. But no, it was good news! They said we were approved and that we needed to go change the power into our name and bring them proof of the transfer and also a money order for our first month's rent by 4:00. So, I hurried and went to the power board and then the bank and Mikey met me at the apartments and we made it there by 4:01. They waited for us, we signed our lease, cleaned it on Thursday and moved in on Friday! God is so faithful! He never leaves us hanging (although He likes to wait to the last minute, at times, to test our faith) and He always provides for us! Our God is an awesome God! It was just another lesson in trusting Him completely! (In the meantime, we were packing and had everything ready to move- by faith. We did not wait until we heard a "Yes" from that apartment. Faith requires action.)

The weekend went by and it was Monday now and we were loving our new place! It was everything we had always wanted in a home, but had never had, since getting married over nine years ago! It had a walk in closet and bathroom in the master bedroom, which we had never had before. It was one story! We have always lived where there were stairs and we don't like stairs, especially with two young kids now, and we were so happy to find a one-story place! It had an open floor plan with the kitchen sink over-looking the living room and towards the kid's room so I could see them playing while I did the dishes. That was one thing I really wanted so I could see them and not worry about them and have to stop and check on them every two minutes. At our house in Knoxville I could never see them from the kitchen when I did dishes. The apartment also had the colors Mikey and I like; the beige walls and tan carpet. It had all new black appliances, which Mikey really likes! We love the black much better than white.

Oh, and after signing the lease that day, Mikey and I saw "777" again, this time together on the back of a car. I think it was a sticker with part of the phone number as "777"! God confirmed it again- third time in the same day that this was His will and this is where He wanted us!

CHAPTER THIRTY-TWO

"A SURPRISE! BABY NUMBER THREE!"

We moved in on March 15th, 2013. We had a very productive week of unpacking and decided to take the kids to Dollywood that next Saturday, opening day, to get a break from unpacking and have fun with them! We went up Friday night and got a hotel since it is too much on the kids to drive there and back in one day. At this time Alexia was now three years and seven months old and Ezekiel was one year and nine months old. Now, we were not planning on getting pregnant at this time, but apparently that night we conceived baby number three without planning it or even trying!

Our little family at Dollywood- The weekend I conceived... again!

Our beautiful Alexia at Dollywood, now 3 years old!

We did try to conceive after Ezekiel turned one and Alexia turned three. We thought if we did have another one, then we wanted this one to be about two years apart from Ezekiel, just like Alexia and Ezekiel were about two years apart. It didn't happen, so we gave up trying and figured we would wait a while and just pray for God's will and timing. Well, after we got back from Dollywood and settled in our new house, I started the Atkin's Diet. I wanted to lose the weight I gained while I was pregnant with Ezekiel. I did it for five days and lost five pounds in those five days. During those five days I was late for my period, but didn't think too much about it. Since having Ezekiel it was normal for me to be one day to six days late. I was still nursing him and my body was still adjusting from having him and trying to get back to "normal". By the fifth day of my diet, I was now eight days late for my period, so I started to wonder if maybe I was pregnant. I asked Mikey if he could pick up a pregnancy test on the way home from Wal*Mart so I could check... just in case!

I was going to wait until that next morning, but I couldn't wait. And if it was positive I wanted Mikey to be there with me when I would find out. Mikey got home and went in the kid's room to play with them. I went into our bathroom to do the test. I waited a couple minutes and checked. Sure enough it was positive! A flood of mixed emotions entered me all at once! I thought for sure it would have been negative and that I was just late, but then again I thought maybe I was. So, I took the stick and went into the room where Mikey was and said, "Are you ready for another adventure?" while I was holding up the pregnancy stick to show him. He said, "Are you serious?!" I said "Yep!" He looked at the stick and gave me a big hug! He was like, "Oh, my gosh, I can't believe it!" He started tearing up. He asked me if

I was okay and what I was thinking and feeling. I told him I was nervous, but excited. I asked him the same. He said he was shocked, but excited!

Alexia had been asking God and praying for a sister for quite some time now. We would tell her, "I don't know. Maybe later on in the future when you are older." She was excited to know there was a baby in my tummy now. We were definitely both excited that God blessed us with another baby. It is a life from God! Of course we were happy. It just wasn't planned by us, so it definitely took us by surprise! We started preparing our hearts and minds to receive another baby in our home and life! Also, at this point in time now, we were completely debt free! We didn't own a home anymore so we had no mortgage or debt. Our car was paid for and we had no credit cards! Debt free and so happy to not be "A slave to the lender." We kept telling ourselves, "We are doing good now and we are ready for another baby!"

Chapter Thirty-Three

"DISCONTENTED!"

After three months of living in our new apartment, in June, I was starting to feel dissatisfied. By dissatisfied I mean I was not happy with my life, as far as what I was "doing" for Jesus. I was full of joy and content in my walk with Jesus, with my husband, and with my kids, but I was tired of being at home all the time and not being out in the "field" laboring for Jesus as He commanded us to do. I was almost feeling guilty. I was starting to be discontented with myself and my life. I really wanted to travel and preach about Jesus and teach other believers the things the Lord has taught me! I had received a prophecy 14 years ago in 2001 that said I would be traveling and that I would have a speaking and singing ministry. The prophecy was from a lady I had never met. The Lord gave her my name and told her about my future. She wrote it down on an index card and gave it to me when their prophetic team came to our church. It said that there would be a time in my early adulthood years where I would be in "a time of isolation, but still in some fellowship".

I've aways wondered when this time would be, and I have thought I was in that season several times before, but now I was sure I was in this time right then. She said it would be a time of preparation, where I would prepare for what God has me to do. Also, to add to this prophetic word, I had a dream a few years back. I don't want to get in to it too much, but I saw us leaving Johnson City in an RV. During this time I had really been thinking about my dream and about getting an RV. Mikey and I have always prayed about it, but those couple weeks during that Summer we had been really taking it seriously and talking about it. At one point it was like something finally clicked in my brain and spirit. It was like all at once I understood what it meant for me (and Mikey) to each personally "prepare for rain". It was like God downloaded what and how our ministry would be and how it would work!

One of my favorite movies is "Facing the Giants". I love all the messages in it, I cry every time I watch it, and I can relate to it. I've always liked the part where Mr. Bridges (the guy praying over the kid's lockers) tells the parable about the two farmers asking God for rain. Then he asks the coach, "Which one are you?" I watch it, then I always pray, "Lord, help me be the one who prepares for the rain!" I asked God, "How do I personally prepare for rain?" What does that mean or look like for me?" I never really knew or understood, except to just keep praying and reading my Bible and doing what I am doing. I felt like He was starting to show me specifics. It was like He told me, "If I've called you to preach and teach, then what do you need to do in order to prepare for that? Write out sermons. Write out teachings from Scripture and from the Greek. Practice speaking your sermons to the mirror and to your family. If I've called you to sing, what do you need to do to prepare for that? Worship me. Practice singing."

It was just like, "Duh, Lacy," but it was exciting. (God didn't say, "Duh". He doesn't talk like that. I was just thinking why hadn't I got that before.) I finally felt like I knew what I needed to do. I had direction now and a sure feeling that I knew this is what God wants me to do! I had a clear view now! I was telling Mikey all of this when he got home from work. I told him how we need to start taking what God has called us to do seriously and that we really need to start preparing for the rain! (Mikey knew this already. I don't want to make it sound like he didn't know and I was just telling him what to do. It was just my passion coming out!) So, while Mikey was at work, this same day, his co-worker told him, "Hey, you should watch this movie called "Faith Like Potatoes." He told Mikey it was a good movie and encouraged us to watch it! So, of course we watched it and it was EXACTLY what the Lord was showing me today and what Mikey and I were talking about. It was about a guy that came to know the Lord and how he prepared for the rain and had faith, and because of that, God brought the rain and blessed him! If you haven't seen it, I'd encourage you to watch it!

Because of all this and getting ideas and direction from God, I wrote a letter the next day, in faith, in hopes to send that following November! The letter was addressed to our family and friends to sponsor us. Why November? Our baby was due in December. We thought we would start traveling when our lease was up in March of 2014. We thought that would give us enough time to bond with our baby after her birth and also enough time to get people to sponsor us. We wanted them to financially support us to travel around the country to preach the gospel to street people and in parks and also stay in cities to help facilitate local outreaches through churches. I also wanted to speak in churches to address the believers with exhortations. I prayed for God's leading for us as this would be a huge step of faith! We needed lots of prayer and guidance!

I am just going to get straight to the point of what was happening. I/we were getting ahead of ourselves. Yes, God did show me/us about preparing for rain. I thought it was in the immediate future though. Yes, God does have a "ministry" for us to do, but it still could have been five or ten years from then. Long story short, we never sent the letter and instead we focused on our third baby that was coming and just kept "preparing" in the mean time. In July of that Summer, we went to the Dr. to find out the gender of our coming baby. Sure enough, like our daughter Alexia had prayed for, it was a girl! A little sister for her! We were so thrilled that it was a girl and were looking forward to her arrival!

Chapter Thirty-Four

"A SHIFT IN FOCUS"

During this Summer, after we realized we were getting ahead of ourselves and ahead of God, He was showing me that I was already "doing" enough. I was a Mom to two kids, which is the hardest job in the world. Maybe not the hardest, but the most important! I was praying and reading His Word and teaching our kids about Him. That was my ministry... for now! That is important to Him. September rolled around and I had a shift in my thinking and in my spirit. I realized that what I was doing was "enough" for now and that is all He wanted me to focus on at that point. I could still be preparing for further, future ministry in the mean time, but just not make it a priority in that season. I had a feeling in my spirit now that we would be moving in the Spring of 2014, around when our lease was up. I know that might sound like, "Duh, of course you have to move when your lease is up!" We didn't have to move though. They said we could just renew our lease in March and stay. Not only did I have a feeling like we would be moving, but I had a feeling it would be out of state. God was preparing my heart. I told Mikey what I was feeling/sensing in my spirit. We started praying about it and asked God if He was wanting us to move out of state or not.

At this same time, in the Fall, Mikey and I were feeling discontented, as far as not having true fellowship with other believers. We were feeling "out of place" and not seeming to find any true connections at the church we were attending, and also at other churches we had visited. As I shared, we had recently moved back from Knoxville and didn't have many friends here now. We tried to reach out to people, serve people, befriend people, etc., but we weren't getting it back. I know we, as Christians, don't do those things just to get it back, but I'm sure you know what I mean though. We were just feeling alone and like no one wanted to be our friend and feeling judged at church for NOT celebrating certain things/holidays and for the decision we make to keep our kids with us at church, etc. We had a lot of hard nights; crying and just longing for friends and fellowship with people that we could relate to and they to us. So, we began praying for God to either connect us somewhere out there in Tennessee or move us!

I really wanted to move because I wanted to start over somewhere new and I didn't really like it in Johnson City that much anyway. I wanted to be in God's will more than my desire to move though, or else we would have taken off a long time ago. We just kept praying that if God wanted us to stay there that He would show us what church to go to and bring us true friends, etc. That wasn't happening. So, we would pray, "Lord, you brought us back to Johnson City for Your reasons. We have been here for a year now... again. If you want us to stay, help us and let us be able to have Christian friends to fellowship with. If our time here is done, please show us and guide us where you want us next!"

One night, while I had personal prayer time of my own, I felt like God told me to look up the number 10. In reality I didn't know what the number 10 meant, but in my spirit it was like I just knew what it meant, if that makes sense. I asked Mikey if he could go on the computer and look it up with me. I just knew in my spirit it meant "Completeness," but I wanted to see for myself. He comes back laughing because it did mean "Completeness". The definition of that number on the site Mikey found is, "A fullness or completeness of something". I also felt the Lord telling me, "Your time here in Tennessee is over. Your time is "Completed" here." I paraphrased a little because I don't remember exactly word for word how it said it. Basically, He was sharing with me that we were done living in Tennessee and that He had somewhere else for us to go. And that didn't mean immediately, but that He was doing a work and getting our pathway ready to move.

In the later Fall, Mikey and I started looking online at different states and places to live and seeing if God would lead us to any particular place. We considered moving to North Carolina or Virginia (to still be close enough to my family to see them, but also closer to the beach and in a new community), or San Diego, California. When we prayed about these places we didn't get an answer. We even put several resumes in for Mikey in San Diego for electrical positions. There were several places hiring for electrician assistants. We never heard back from any of those. Then, even though we really wanted to move to San Diego to be by the beach and around fun things to do for the kids, Mikey didn't want to move there because of how bad California is getting. They are passing ungodly laws and trying to outlaw homeschooling and we don't want to live somewhere where I can't homeschool our kids.

So, Winter came and we put everything aside and I had my baby and we focused on her and on me getting better and taking time to heal for a couple months. Our baby girl was due on December 11th, which is on one of my sister's birth day, but she came two days "early" and was born on Monday, December 9th, 2013 at 5:35 a.m.! She weighed 8 lbs, 9 oz and was 20 inches long. She was perfect and this was the best and fastest labor by far compared to my other two! I started labor Sunday night after the kids went to sleep and then went to the hospital at 1:00 a.m. and was at 5 cm already. I progressed really fast and started pushing. My water broke as I was starting to push her out and then she came out shortly after my water broke (or should I say burst on the Dr. LOL)! It was much better waiting on God and His timing this time, instead of being induced and trying to make it happen earlier. And thanks to my friend, Julie, who came out at midnight to help us and watch our kids for us at the hospital! It was a really great experience and I was so thankful to God for a shorter labor and delivery and for not having her come late to where I would need Pitocin again.

Ezekiel with me at the hospital!

Me and Mikey with our sweet baby, Serenity Joy! One month old.

A few months after I had my baby, those same feelings started coming back again; about not fitting in, not connecting anywhere, etc. One day one of Mikey's old friends, Brandon, called him to see how we were doing. They talked a little while and Brandon was telling Mikey what an awesome job he had and how he was leading worship at their church, etc. At this point Mikey was looking for another job (even if it was a new job in Johnson City), so I kiddingly, but also a little serious I guess, laughed and said, "Mikey, ask him if his work place is hiring (since he was saying how great of a job it is)!" Mikey did ask and Brandon (who lives in Arizona) said, "Yes, they are getting ready to hire." There was a guy not doing his job there so they were going to let him go. Brandon said, "Hey, I'll put a good word in for you to my boss and see what happens and I will call you and let you know." At this point we were half joking, but just said, "Okay." We prayed about it and were ready to leave and make the move, but we just put it aside and waited to hear back from Brandon.

Well, I think about three weeks went by and we hadn't heard anything so we just kind of forgot about it and kept praying for God to show us where He wanted us. So, then we were talking about moving again and God gave Mikey a dream. I am not going to get into the dream and what God showed him, but God made it clear to Mikey when to put his two weeks notice in. A couple weeks later, what was in Mikey's dream happened. He knew that was the timing. So, he did put in his two weeks notice at that point with faith that God was providing something else. (He/we wouldn't quit just to quit, because that would be foolishness, not faith, but by the Lord's leading he quit.) After this, I believe that same week, on Friday, his friend Brandon called him again and said, "Guess what? That guy got fired and we are coming into our busy season and my boss is going to be hiring." He called back and gave Mikey the phone number for the HR lady and told him to send his resume to her. That was Friday night and she wasn't in the office until Monday. So, Mikey called and talked to her on Monday and got her e-mail address. We prayed over his resume and e-mailed it over to her! She got it and gave it to the boss. The boss called Mikey and gave him a phone interview. It wasn't even long into the interview when this boss (who is a Mormon by the way) decided that he really liked Mikey and his personality and he hired him! He asked Mikey when he could start. Mikey said, "Well, I still have one more week left at the job I currently have until my two weeks notice are up. Then it will take us at least four days to drive there. So, I can start on that following Monday." The boss said, "Okay, I'll see you then!"

So, we packed that weekend and during Mikey's last week of work and then that following weekend the movers came and picked up our stuff! We started driving that Monday, April 14th! As far as a home goes, Brandon's wife was a property manager for a house in Buckeye, Arizona. It was a four bedroom, three bathroom, two-story house! It was up for rent. We weren't sure about it at first because we didn't want a place with stairs because of our two littlest babies. We still prayed about it. We wanted to get a one story apartment with no stairs that would be a little more inexpensive than a house for us, but we felt that the Lord wanted us in that house.

The property manager told us that another couple was wanting to rent the house. So, we were kind of waiting to see if they were for sure going to get it or not. We really had peace about the house, but not about the apartment. We knew if the house was where God wanted us that He would make the way for us to get it. Also, one other thing. Mine and Mikey's favorite Bible verse that we based our marriage on is Ephesians 2:22 and the first three numbers of this house's address were "222"! That was like another confirmation to us from the Lord. When we started looking for a place in Buckeye, Arizona, once we knew we were going to be moving there, I told Mikey, "If you or we find a house with the address of "222" in it, then we know that is the right house!" I was kidding because we like that number, but I felt inclined to look for a house with "222" in the address anyway! This house had it!

There was also something else about the name of the street I felt God show me, but I am not going to share it on here because that would give away our address and I don't feel that would be a smart idea. Anyway, we had faith and sure enough the couple backed out and we got the house! It was ready for us to move into. Our apartment here was easy to move out of, too. Our lease expired in March, so now we were living there on a month to month basis and we just told them we would be moving out on the 17th, which was only two days after our monthly renewal on the 15th. They okayed it.

There were also other things the Lord confirmed to us. The Lord spoke to my husband about actually moving to Arizona and confirmed it to him. God also showed Mikey some things through a "Joseph" movie that confirmed where He wanted us and that it *was* His will for Mikey to take the job at Greenleaf Pest Control that his friend helped him get! He confirmed it to us. We shared it with my family and then we left.

Chapter Thirty-Five

"Arizona!"

It is now March of 2015 as I am finishing up my book to print and publish now! We have been in Arizona for 11 months and are absolutely loving it! God has connected us with a couple of sets of awesome, married, and godly authentic Christian couples! We have been able to fellowship with them and have that true bond and unity with them that Mikey and I were craving in Johnson City, but couldn't get. (I just want to clarify- we did have two sets of good friends in Johnson City, but they each had four kids and they were just really busy, so it was hard to meet consistently). God has set Mikey up with some divine appointments at work already. Mikey has also been able to witness to, pray with, and encourage so many people at the places where he has worked- it has been so cool! When we first came here we were going to our friend's church at New Foundation in Goodyear. We made some connections there and we liked it and liked the Pastor. After some time though, we felt the Lord tell us that was not where He wanted us permanently.

When we got here, we also connected with a family in Gilbert, Arizona, to start a home group/home church with them. We connected with them through "The Fuel Project" online. If you have never heard of "The Fuel Project" by Mark Fairly and the Apologetics Group, I highly encourage you to look it up on YouTube and watch it! It is very, very good! Mark shares about how we need to know our enemy in the "Know Your Enemy" series. He teaches basic discipleship in the "Stay Free" series. And he goes back to the book of Acts to define how the "church" should be today in "The Restless Church" series. They are all wonderful teachings that have helped my husband and I grow tremendously in our walk with Jesus! Visit www. thefuelproject.org to glean from these awesome studies! Anyway, Mark's purpose in doing these series, and especially the one called, "The Restless Church" is to connect believers all over America and all over the world. He wants Christians to find other Christians in their area and be able to connect and start home groups together. That is what we did. We found this family that felt the same way Mikey and I did and they wanted to start a home church and so did we and we joined up with them and now we have a home church!

This home church has been amazing! We have met with them for 11 months now, since we first got here. It has grown. Another Jewish lady started coming. My Mom and Dad just moved here to Arizona, too, in February, and now they come. Our neighbor comes now, too. We are just praying for God's will and for Him to do what He wants through us and through our home church! I didn't get into this previously, but Mikey and I were and are kind of "over" church. Let me explain. I know this American mentally of what a Christian is, is that you have to belong to a church and attend that church every Sunday. If you tell someone you're a Christian, the first question out of their mouth is usually, "Oh, where do you go to church?" Then, depending on where you go, they get more of an idea about what you believe or what kind of person you are. I don't want to be known by "what" church I go to. According to the Bible, "we" are the church. The church is a "we", not a "what". When we become Christians and choose to follow Jesus, we are the church! It is not a building. The church IS the body of Christ!

Mikey and I have gotten so tired of typical "church". I'm not going to say everywhere, but most places we have gone to church or churches we have visited are all pretty much the same. Most of them are programmed, pre-planned, routinized, and follow the same format. All, but one we have been to do worship first- typically like three fast songs, two slow songs, then announcements, then preaching for 30-60 minutes. Most churches nowadays are also timed. There might be multiple services, so they feel they have to time the service in order to get the people in and out faster. It's like twenty minutes of worship, ten minutes of announcements or/and cool videos, and thirty minutes of preaching, and you're out of there! And don't forget your coffee on the way out. There is no time to have real church. There is no time to ask questions and teach each other. It just a fast-paced service that doesn't allow much room, if any room, for the Spirit of God to move. Mikey and I have witnessed it first hand, particularly two times, at two different churches, where the Holy Spirit was moving and doing a work, but then because of "time", the Pastor came up and stopped the move of the Spirit and "went on" with the service to keep in time with their schedule! That is so sad to watch and it grieved mine and Mikey's spirit and of course it grieved God's Spirit. He wanted to do a work in His children, but the Pastors wouldn't allow it. They are so focused on their own schedule and on their own teaching, that they move on, leaving God behind, and doing the service by themselves, in their own strength.

That is not how "church" should be. According to the Bible, and especially the book of Acts, the "church" was in "one accord" and also met from "house to house". We should be praying and waiting on the Lord and allowing His spirit to guide the meeting and lead His people. All this Americanized church that is pre-planned does not allow for His people to wait on Him. "So continuing daily with one accord in the temple, and breaking bread from house to house, they ate their food with gladness and simplicity of heart, praising God and having favor with all the people. And the Lord added to the church daily those who were being saved." Acts 2:46 & 47 NKJV And in Hebrews 3:13 NKJV, "But exhort one another daily, while it is called "Today", lest any of you be hardened through the deceitfulness of sin." We are also supposed to be exhorting each other, not having one man preach to us/at us, but exhorting each other. And Colossians 3:16 NIV, "Let the message of Christ dwell among you richly as you teach and admonish one another with all wisdom through psalms, hymns, and songs from the Spirit, singing to God with gratitude in your hearts." We are called to teach and admonish each other! Again, not listening to a sermon for a half hour, but teaching each other. You can't do that in any church service that I know of. The only way to do that is in a home group setting where you have the time and freedom to wait on the Lord and then teach others as He leads you.

I am not bashing the church. God still uses it to get the gospel out there and to bring in and teach new believers, but we need to go beyond that. How are we "making disciples" if there is no one on one intimate connection? Disciples aren't likely to be made hearing a sermon once a week. We need to take time to make healthy friendships and mentor people. I love our home group because we can do that. When we meet, we take four to five hours at a time to fellowship, pray, wait on the Lord (Holy Spirit), have some time of praise and/ or worship, we get to teach each other, encourage each other, eat a meal together, do communion, etc. It is not rushed or pre-planned. And it is never the same. We do different things each time and it doesn't have to be in the same order. It is very free. I get much more out of that than attending "a church".

Also, a lot of churches now preach the salvation message, which is great, but they are "peaching to the choir". It is hard to get new converts when you are preaching to Christians who are already saved! The "church" must go out to the unbelievers, and that is the role of evangelists. They get the people "saved" and then bring them into church where they should be discipled. However, nowadays that doesn't seem to happen much. The preacher tries to get the church saved every week and then there seems to be a lack of admonishing, equipping, training, etc. and therefore a lack of "sending out" the laborers into the field. Again, not every church, but from what Mikey and I have seen in the majority of the churches we've visited or been a part of there seems to be a lack of training. Don't feel guilty if you don't like going to church. It could be that your spirit is just not satisfied with what is happening at church every week. Just ask God why you are feeling that way and let Him lead you.

Christianity is not about going to church on Sundays. Our society has it all wrong. It is about a real, genuine relationship with Jesus Christ, God, and the Holy Spirit! You don't have to go to church every week to be a Christian or if you already are a Christian. That could turn in to a "works" thing. If you feel guilty because you missed a Sunday, it is probably your own thoughts or the enemy. If God tells you to go, that is a different story, but if you are just going to go every week because you think you have to and you miss a week, it is okay. Don't let legalism get the best of you and make you feel guilty. The Bible says in Hebrews 10:25 NKJV "Not forsaking the assembling of ourselves together, as is the manner of some, but exhorting one another, and so much the more as you see the Day approaching." You pray and ask the Holy Spirit what that means. I don't think it necessarily means, "You have to go to church." I believe it means you need to continually meet and "assemble" together with other believers for fellowship and to exhort one another.

This Christian walk is a journey; an adventure. We are always learning and growing in the knowledge of Him! Now, we eagerly await expectantly for what He will do next in our lives! It is always something new. This walk isn't easy, but it is sure worth it! I encourage each of you that are reading my book to seek God with all your heart, mind, will, emotions, etc.! It says if we seek Him, we will find Him! He has plans for you! Let Him lead your life. Give it all to Him! If you have never asked Jesus into your heart, then, "Today is the day of salvation!" Just simply pray to God and invite Jesus into your heart. Ask Him to forgive you of your sins. Repent for sinning against God. Ask Jesus to be Lord of your life and submit yourself and your life to Him and His authority! Thank Him for dying on the cross for you! Invite the Holy Spirit in to your heart and spirit to help you and to lead and guide you. It really is that simple. But count the cost first. The cost of following Jesus is your life. You give up your plans to follow His plans, which by the way are much better! His plans for me were much better than the plans I had for myself! He loves you and wants what is best for you! Trust Him today... even with your life! Be blessed!

CHAPTER THIRTY-SIX

"IN CLOSING..."

Just in closing, I wanted to talk about my children. I know I mentioned their births, but did not get to talk much about them with everything else I shared. Alexia Jade is now five years old, Ezekiel Daniel is now three years old, and Serenity Joy is now one year old! Yes, they are all about two years apart and keep me very busy at home! Alexia is in Kindergarten now. I homeschool her at home! Mikey and I feel it is very clear in God's Word for us as the parents to, "Train up a child in the way he/she should go, and when he is old he will not depart from it," Proverbs 22:6 KJV. We feel strongly that is is our role as their parents to train them up ourselves, in every way; spiritually, educationally, financially, mentally, emotionally, etc. and not have other teachers and/or daycare providers, family or friends do it for us. If we trust our kids in the care of someone else, then we have no idea what those teachers/daycare providers will be teaching our kids. There is no guarantee that they will be learning what is right and Biblical. We also wouldn't be able to guard their hearts and minds.

I have heard that in some places and states they are even starting to teach Kindergarten kids "sex education", teaching that "homosexuality is a choice", and teaching about "evolution". I don't want my kids learning any of that. They need to learn the truth. When Alexia was three (almost four) we thought about enrolling her in a program in Tennessee called "Head Start". It is a pre-school program that she would have gone to for four hours a day to learn basic letters, colors, patterns, etc. and therefore have a "head start" when it was time for her to start Kindergarten. We filled out the paperwork for her to go and they had one spot available and they said she could have it. When we prayed about it, the Lord made it clear to us to not put her in that program. He made it clear to us that these were our children, and that it was our responsibility to teach them ourselves. I remember thinking back then, "Well, this is the thing to do though. I've got to get my child in this program so she will be smart and do good in school." There was such a temptation there to do just what "the normal thing" is and what everyone else does and just put my child in school, but I had to be obedient to the Lord and not to what society wants for my child. It is much more better and beneficial for her and our other kids to have a firm foundation spiritually, than academically. I know a school system will not give them that. The Lord also reminded me that, "I am well capable to teach my children", and that "He will give me the strength and grace I need" to do it.

So, all that said, Alexia is finishing up her Kindergarten year now and will start first grade with me this Summer! She is already reading short words and basic sentences! She can also do basic addition, is memorizing Bible Scriptures, and learning all about God's creation! I teach her from a Christian curriculum called, "My Father's World". It is all about seeing the world through God's eyes. It has been great so far! I love it! The thing I love most is that she learns a new characteristic about God, our Father, every week! For example, one week she learned that we are safe in God. She learned about how the kangaroo Mommy and its baby is like us with God; like when we are hidden in Him, He keeps us safe, just as a mommy kangaroo keeps its baby safe when it is hidden in her pouch. Anyway, I recommend it to homeschooling mothers! Great curriculum!

Alexia loves it, too. She also wanted me to homeschool her. I feel better knowing she is at home with me and I am keeping her safe spiritually and physically. Anyone can do it. Don't think you can't just because you work or don't have the time or money. If you want to homeschool your kid(s), ask God to help you and make a way. Maybe quit your job or cut back on hours or take opposite shifts from your husband. God makes a way when there seems to be no way. Since I was pregnant with our first daughter/child, I have not worked and my husband has worked full time, and even two jobs at a time before, so that I can stay home with our kids. We feel it is really that important to take time to be with our kids and to raise our kids. God has made that possible. It is also our choice. We can choose for me to work and have more money, but we choose to be with our kids more than we want more money. We have had to sacrifice some things in order for me to stay home, but it is truly worth it. Since it is in God's word for a Mom to stay home and take care of her kids and her house, He honors that and always provides for us. Even at times when Mikey has not made enough, He always sends someone to give us money and He has taught us that He is our Provider, not Mikey. We have to trust Him and let Him be though. If we strived to do it ourselves and both worked and just focused on more money, then we would just wear ourselves out, and not to mention, we would be proving to God that we don't trust Him to meet our needs.

Back to Alexia. She is my "Compassion" kid. She has many great qualities, but the one that sticks out to me the most is her compassion. She has compassion on me when I am hurt or sick and she has so much compassion for others when she sees them out in public, sick or hurting. I know God will use that compassion in her for her to reach out to those people. She is also my little evangelist. Everywhere we go now, she says, "Mommy, can you ask her/him if she/he knows Jesus." I say, "Okay", and I ask them. She also asks kids on the playground if they are Christians and if they know Jesus! It is so awesome to have a daughter that is not afraid to tell people about Jesus and who pushes me to do the same! She just recently accepted Jesus into her heart, last month, on March 16th! It was a joyous occasion and we will be baptizing her soon!

Alexia- My little model!

On to Ezekiel. He is almost in Pre-school now. I will be homeschooling him with the "ABCJesus Loves Me" pre-school curriculum (same one I did for Alexia for pre-school). I will start that with him this Summer after he turns four. He is my absolutely sweet, loving little boy and my only boy. He also has many great qualities, but the one that sticks out to me the most is his love. He has so much love and affection for me, his Daddy, and his sisters! I love watching him wake up in the morning and give his sisters hugs and kisses! He is very affectionate, the most affectionate out of all three of our kids. He always kisses me and Mikey and he wants to cuddle with me at night to go to sleep. In the morning he says, "Good morning, Sister" to Alexia and "Good morning, Whenity" to Serenity, (he can't say the "S" yet). When Mikey gets home from work, he runs to him, hugs and kisses him and says, "Daddy, I'm so glad you're home," or/and "It is so good to see you!" He is super cute. He also just recently accepted Jesus into his heart the day before Alexia did, on March 15th! We will be baptizing him, too! I am so excited! He and Alexia are best friends! He is still transitioning to make Serenity his best friend, too! Now that she is walking and getting bigger, it gets tough for a three year old to share everything, including Mommy, but he is doing good.

Ezekiel- my happy and loving little boy!

As for Serenity, her name says it all. Serenity Joy. She is peaceful (serene) and joyful. The quality that stands out most to me, in her, is her joy! She is so funny and makes everyone smile and laugh. She is such a character already at only 15 months old. She is very content and happy and does her own thing, but is also learning now how to play with her older siblings. Overall, the three of them do great together and have so much fun! Not to mention, they are all the cutest kids ever! Mikey and I love each of them so much and couldn't imagine life without them!

Serenity Joy- One Year Old!

As far as Mikey and I go, we are happier than ever! We have been married for over 11 years now and have become so strong together from all the hard things we had to go through. I wouldn't go back and change anything because I know that God has used it all to make me and Mikey better people and more loving to each other and others. We are just excited to be on this adventure together and make this journey, called "Life" together!

Whoever said, "Accept Jesus in your heart and become a Christian, and all your problems will go away" was wrong. To be a Christian is not the "easy way". It is the hard and narrow way that few choose. No wonder Jesus said, "If you want to follow Me, you need to count the cost..." (Read Luke 14). It costs us everything to follow Jesus- our own life, our own will, our everything, but is absolutely worth it! His plan for us is far better than our own plans for us. His ways are better than our ways. When we learn to truly submit to Him and His lordship, we find true freedom. He makes the way for us. He blesses us. He provides for us. What better exchange for our lives is there than that of following Jesus?

Now, back to me and Mikey. There are two "new" opportunities before us right now, and specifically for Mikey. We are praying about them and anticipating something great from them- from God! It is always a fun adventure when we follow Jesus. He always has something new for us to learn and to be blessed in. I am and we are so excited to see how these two opportunities unfold before us as we seek Him. Not to mention that I am now getting to publish my first book at this same time as well! This was one of my goals that the Lord led me to do and it is happening now! We are so excited! Such a fun season right now! I am sure I will also be writing another book, titled "My Testimony Part 2" in a couple of years to continue sharing with you all the awesome things God will do in our lives as we follow Him!

I encourage you if you don't know Him today to invite Him into your heart. Ask Him to forgive you of your sins. Repent of your sins. Submit your life to Him. Submit to His lordship. You won't regret it. If you are not sure if this is all real of if God is even real, then ask Him to show Himself to you. "If you ask, He will answer. If you seek, He will be found. If you knock, He will open the door." (Read Matthew 7) Say, "God if you are real, prove it. Show yourself to me. Show me you are real." He will!

Peace to all of you from the Lord Jesus Christ!

P.S. For more information on anything I discussed in my book or if you have any questions for me about myself or about knowing Jesus, find me on Youtube at Lacy Megan on my own personal channel and click the "Subscribe" button! I have teachings on there about "Salvation", the "Holy Spirit", what it means to be a "New Creation", what "Born Again" means, etc. My husband has a couple of awesome recipes on there, too! We would be happy to connect with you and hear from you! You can also find me on Facebook under Lacy Megan to see more pictures of my gorgeous family!

I also love photography and have done some photography on the side, so connect with me if you need photos done!

Chapter Thirty-Seven

"EXTRA"

MINE AND MY FAMILY'S NAMES AND MEANINGS:

Names do have a meaning and to get more of an idea of who I am and who Mikey is, read what our names mean. We truly are like our names. I am "joyful", Mikey is "like the Lord", in how he loves unconditionally, etc. I am stubborn and persistent, which is where my "Victorious Spirit" comes from I guess!

LACY MEGAN
Lacy- Language/Cultural Origin: Latin
Inherent Meaning: "Joyful"
Spiritual Connotation: "Filled With Praise"
Scripture: Psalm 98:4 RSV
"Make a joyful noise to the Lord, all the earth;
break forth into joyous song and sing praises!"

Megan- Language/Cultural Origin: Welsh
Inherent Meaning: "Mighty"
Spiritual Connotation: "Victorious Spirit"
Scripture: Isaiah 2:5 NRSV
"O house of Jacob, come,
let us walk in the light of the Lord!"

MICHAEL JASON

Michael (Mikey)- Language/Cultural Origin: Hebrew

Inherent Meaning: "Who Is Like God?"

Spiritual Connotation: "Esteemed"

Scripture: Exodus 15:11 NKJV

"Who is like You, O Lord, among the gods?

Who is like You, glorious in holiness,

fearful in praises, doing wonders?"

Jason- Language/Cultural Origin: Greek

Inherent Meaning: "Healer"

Spiritual Connotation: "Benevolent"

Scripture: Luke 6:45 NKJV

"A good man out of the good treasure

of his heart brings forth good... For out of the

abundance of the heart his mouth speaks."

My beautiful children!

ALEXIA JADE

Alexia- Language/Cultural Origin: Hungarian

Inherent Meaning: "Defender of Mankind"

Spiritual Connotation: "Benefactor"

Scripture: Isaiah 1:7 RSV

"Learn to do good; seek justice, correct oppression;
defend the fatherless, plead for the widow."

Jade- Language/Cultural Origin: Spanish

Inherent Meaning: "Precious Gem"

Spiritual Connotation: "Priceless"

Scripture: James 1:7 NKJV

"Every good gift and every perfect gift is from above,
and comes down from the Father of lights, with whom
there is no variation or shadow of turning."

Alexia Jade- 5

EZEKIEL DANIEL

Ezekiel- Language/Cultural Origin: Hebrew

Inherent Meaning: "Whom God Makes Strong"

Spiritual Connotation: "God Is My Strength"

Scripture: 1 Corinthians 2:12 NKJV

"Now we have received, not the spirit of the world, but the Spirit who is from God."

Daniel- Language/Cultural Origin: Hebrew

Inherent Meaning: "God Is My Judge"

Spiritual Connotation: "Discerning"

Scripture: Psalm 119:142 NKJV

"Your righteousness is an everlasting righteousness, and Your law is truth."

Ezekiel Daniel- 3

SERENITY JOY

Serenity- Language/Cultural Origin: Latin

Inherent Meaning: "Secure"

Spiritual Connotation: "Content"

Scripture: 1 Corinthians 2:12 NCV

"Now we did not receive the spirit of the world,

but we received the Spirit that is from God

so that we can know all that God has given us."

Joy- Language/Cultural Origin: Latin

Inherent Meaning: "Joyful"

Spiritual Connotation: "Follower of Truth"

Scripture: Psalm 119:105 NKJV

"Your Word is a lamp to my feet

and a light to my path."

Serenity Joy- 1

Family photo- All five of us!
Lacy-30, Mikey-28, Alexia- 5,
Ezekiel- 3, Serenity- 8 months old!